Three Pacific Northwest Poets
William Stafford, Richard Hugo,
and David Wagoner

Twayne's United States Authors Series

Warren French, Editor
University College of Swansea, Wales

TUSAS 506

Three Pacific Northwest Poets
William Stafford, Richard Hugo, and David Wagoner

By Sanford Pinsker

Franklin and Marshall College

Twayne Publishers
A Division of G.K. Hall & Co. • Boston

Three Pacific Northwest Poets:
William Stafford, Richard Hugo, and David Wagoner

Sanford Pinsker

Copyright © 1987 by G.K. Hall & Co.
All Rights Reserved
Published by Twayne Publishers
A Division of G.K. Hall & Co.
70 Lincoln Street
Boston, Massachusetts 02111

Copyediting supervised by Lewis DeSimone
Book production by Marne B. Sultz
Book design by Barbara Anderson

Typeset in 11 pt. Garamond
by P&M Typesetting, Inc., Waterbury, Connecticut

Printed on permanent/durable acid-free paper
and bound in the United States of America

Library of Congress Cataloging in Publication Data

Pinsker, Sanford.
    Three Pacific northwest poets.

    (Twayne's United States authors series ; TUSAS 506)
    Bibliography: p. 132
    Includes index.
    1. American poetry—Northwest, Pacific—History and
criticism.   2. American poetry—20th century—History
and criticism.   3. Stafford, William—Criticism and
interpretation.   4. Hugo, Richard F.—Criticism and
interpretation.   5. Wagoner, David—Criticism and
interpretation.   6. Northwest, Pacific—Intellectual
life.   I. Title.   II. Series.
PS282.P56   1987   811'.54'099795   87-43
ISBN 0-8057-7500-5

To Theodore Roethke (1908–1963) —
In gratitude for his work, and life.

Contents

About the Author

Sanford Pinsker is Professor of English at Franklin and Marshall College. He did his undergraduate work at Washington and Jefferson College and received his doctorate from the University of Washington. Professor Pinsker is the author of *The Schlemiel as Metaphor* (1971), *The Languages of Joseph Conrad* (1978), *Between Two Worlds: The American Novel in the 1960s* (1978), *Critical Essays on Philip Roth* (1982), *Conversations with Contemporary American Writers* (1985), as well as several collections of his own poems.

Preface

William Stafford, Richard Hugo, and David Wagoner are highly individual poets whose thematic and technical interests vary widely. The three do, however, share a relationship to the general development of contemporary American poetry and to the northwestern milieu they have for many years called their home. To an extent, it is geography that accounts for their inclusion in this study. But it is more than that. Each has produced a substantial body of important poetry that has received less critical attention than it deserves.

Furthermore, their work has special interests and attractions for me. As a graduate student at the University of Washington, I was privileged to study with David Wagoner and to watch collections like *Staying Alive* or *Riverbed* as they grew poem by poem by poem. As I have come to realize in completing this book, the University of Washington was an exciting place to be in the mid-sixties. Richard Hugo had, of course, already established himself at the University of Montana, but his work was much talked about in Seattle. William Stafford I met later, and found myself returning to Portland, Oregon, whenever there was a chance we might get together.

The brief introduction underlines the abiding influence of Theodore Roethke on poets of the Pacific Northwest, at the same time that it suggests the difficulties with such an equation. However fiercely individual Stafford, Hugo, and Wagoner may be, they exist in a context, in a firmly grounded time and place. The introduction, then, provides this context for the individual surveys to follow, each a monograph-length treatment of one of the poets. Each survey begins with a biographical sketch and then proceeds to a book-by-book analysis, paying special attention to describing and assessing characteristic themes and techniques and consistently offering close readings of representative poems to support general observations.

My thanks to William Stafford, Richard Hugo, and David Wagoner for their help and encouragement of this project, for their letters in response to specific questions, and for providing materials I could not otherwise have obtained. Franklin and Marshall College was, as always, generous in its research assistance. Special thanks to Jody

Gladding and Charles Molesworth, to my wife, Ann, and to my editor, Warren French; each read portions of the manuscript and made valuable suggestions for its improvement.

Sanford Pinsker

Franklin and Marshall College

Acknowledgments

Grateful acknowledgment is made to Harper & Row, Publishers, Inc. to quote specified selections from *Stories That Could Be True: New and Collected Poems* by William Stafford. Copyright © 1977 by William Stafford. *American Poetry Review* gave its kind permission to reprint my interview with William Stafford entitled "Finding Out What the World Is Trying to Be," which appeared in its issue of vol. 4, no. 4. *Northwest Review* permitted me to quote from William Stafford's "Into the Cold World: Leaving the World" and "On Being Local," which appeared in its issue of vol. 13, no. 3.

Quotations from Donna Gerstenberger's *Richard Hugo* are reprinted by permission of the publisher, Boise State University's Western Writers Series.

Thanks to Indiana University Press for permission to quote from *Collected Poems, 1956–1976* by David Wagoner.

Grateful acknowledgment is made for reprinting the following selections: *Making Certain It Goes On: The Collected Poems of Richard Hugo,* by permission of W. W. Norton & Company, Inc. Copyright © 1984 by The Estate of Richard Hugo; *The Triggering Town: Lectures and Essays on Poetry and Writing,* by Richard Hugo, by permission of W. W. Norton & Company, Inc. Copyright © 1979 by W. W. Norton & Company, Inc.; *White Center: Poems by Richard Hugo,* by permission of W. W. Norton & Company, Inc. Copyright © 1980 by Richard Hugo; *The Right Madness on Skye: Poems by Richard Hugo,* by permission of W. W. Norton & Company, Inc. Copyright © 1980 by Richard Hugo.

Chronologies

William Stafford

1914   Born 17 January in Hutchinson, Kansas. Father: Earl Ingersoll Stafford; mother: Ruby Mayer Stafford. (Raised in Kansas—Hutchinson, Wichita, Liberal, Garden City, El Dorado.)

1937   A.B., University of Kansas.

1942–1946   Conscientious objector held in camps in Arkansas, California, and Illinois.

1944   Marries Dorothy Hope Frantz.

1946   M.A., University of Kansas.

1947   *Down in My Heart* (autobiography).

1948–1950   Instructor in English, Lewis and Clark College.

1950–1954   Student assistant, University of Iowa.

1954   Ph.D., University of Iowa.

1954–1955   Assistant professor in English, Manchester College, Indiana.

1955–1956   Assistant professor in English, San Jose State College, California.

1956–1980   Assistant, associate, professor, Lewis and Clark College.

1960   *West of Your City.*

1962   *Traveling Through the Dark* (National Book Award).

1966   *The Rescued Year.*

1970   *Allegiances.*

1973   *Someday, Maybe.*

1976   *Braided Apart* (with Kim Robert Stafford).

1977   *Smoke's Way.*

1978   *Writing the Australian Crawl: Views on the Writer's Vocation* (prose).

1980   *Things That Happen Where There Aren't Any People*; retires from Lewis and Clark College.

1981 *Sometimes Like a Legend.*

1982 *A Glass Face in the Rain.*

1983 *Segues: A Correspondence in Poetry* (with Marvin Bell).

Richard (Franklin) Hugo

1919 Born 21 December in Seattle, Washington. Father: Herbert F. Hugo; mother: Esther Monk Hugo. (Raised in Seattle, Washington.)

1943–1945 Serves in U.S. Army Air Forces as a bombardier (First Lieutenant) in the Mediterranean theater; receives Distinguished Flying Cross and Air Medal.

1948 B.A., University of Washington, Seattle.

1951 Marries Barbara Williams.

1951–1963 Works for Boeing Aircraft Corporation, Seattle, Washington.

1952 M.A., University of Washington, Seattle.

1961 *A Run of Jacks.*

1964 Appointed professor of English at University of Montana, Missoula; collaborates on *Five Poets of the Pacific.*

1965 *Death of the Kapowsin Tavern.*

1966 Divorced from Barbara Williams; receives Northwest Writers Award.

1967–1968 Receives Rockefeller Foundation creative writing grant.

1969 *Good Luck in Cracked Italian.*

1973 *The Lady in Kicking Horse Reservoir.* (Nominated for a National Book Award.)

1974 Marries Ripley Schemm.

1975 *What Thou Lovest Well, Remains American.* (Nominated for a National Book Award.)

1977 *31 Letters and 13 Dreams.*

1979 *Selected Poems. The Triggering Town: Lectures and Essays on Poetry and Writing* (prose).

1980 *White Center. The Right Madness on Skye.*

1981 *Death and the Good Life* (mystery novel).

1982   Dies of leukemia, 22 October in Seattle, Washington.

1983   *The Hitler Diaries* (novel). *Sea Lanes Out* (poetry).

1984   *Making Certain It Goes On.*

David (Russell) Wagoner

1926   Born 5 June in Massillon, Ohio. Father: Walter Siffert Wagoner; mother: Ruth Calder Wagoner. (Raised in Whiting, Indiana; attends school in Hammond, Indiana.)

1944–1946   Midshipman in NROTC.

1946   A.B., Pennsylvania State University.

1949   M.A., Indiana University.

1949–1950   Instructor, DePauw University.

1950   Marries Elizabeth Arensman, divorced 1953.

1950–1953   Instructor, Pennsylvania State University.

1953   *Dry Sun, Dry Wind.*

1954   *The Man in the Middle*; instructor, University of Washington, subsequently full professor in 1966.

1955   *Money Money Money.*

1956   Guggenheim Fellow in fiction, travels to Spain, France, and England.

1958   *Rock. A Place to Stand.*

1961   Marries Patricia Lee Parrott, divorced 1982.

1963   *The Nesting Ground.*

1964   Ford Fellowship in drama; playwright in residence, Seattle Repertory Theatre.

1965   *The Escape Artist* (fiction).

1966   *Staying Alive.* Becomes editor of *Poetry Northwest.*

1967   Zabel Prize, *Poetry* (Chicago); award from National Institute of Arts and Letters.

1968   *Baby, Come on Inside.*

1968   Elliston Lecturer in Modern Poetry, University of Cincinnati.

1969 *New and Selected Poems;* National Council on the Arts Award.

1970 *Where is My Wandering Boy Tonight?* (fiction).

1971 Tours Greece, Turkey, and Lebanon for the U.S. Information Agency, reading poems and lecturing on American poetry.

1972 *Riverbed; Straw for the Fire.*

1974 *Sleeping in the Woods;* Blumenthal-Leviton-Blonder Prize. *Poetry* (Chicago).

1975 *Tracker;* two Fels Prizes from Coordinating Council of Literary Magazines, one for poetry, one for editing.

1976 *Whole Hog. Collected Poems, 1956–1976.*

1977 Tietjens Prize, *Poetry* (Chicago); nominated for National Book Award in poetry; Pushcart Prize in poetry.

1978 Elected one of twelve chancellors of Academy of American poets. *Who Shall Be the Sun?*; editor of Princeton University Press Contemporary Poetry Series for three-year term.

1979 *In Broken Country*; Pacific Northwest Booksellers Award for excellence in writing.

1980 Nominated for the American Book Award in poetry; Sherwood Anderson Award in fiction; English-speaking Union Prize, *Poetry* (Chicago); *The Hanging Garden* (fiction).

1981 *Landfall.*

1982 Marries Robin Heather Seyfried; feature film based on *The Escape Artist* produced by Francis Ford Coppola, directed by Caleb Deschanel, released by Orion Pictures-Warner Brothers.

1983 Pushcart Prize in poetry; editor of University of Missouri Press Breakthrough Series; *First Light.*

1985 Charles Angoff Prize, *The Literary Review.*

Chapter One
Theodore Roethke and the Pacific Northwest Poets

Much has happened since Theodore Roethke joined the English Department at the University of Washington in Seattle. The year was 1947, and in his notebooks Roethke remembers it this way:

. . . when I came out to Seattle, the head of my department said "Ted, we don't quite know what to do with you: you're the only serious practicing poet within 1500 miles." I sort of was given to understand that I had a status between—if it were Oklahoma—between a bank-robber and a Congressman.[1]

Granted, Roethke was a poet around whom apocrypha clustered, and he was not above doing some Whitmanian advertising for himself. His voracious appetite, his compulsive brag-and-swagger, had a peculiarly American ring. His was a life and an art dedicated to taking on *everything*. Which is to say, there may be more crowing than truth in the words Roethke put into his chairman's mouth.

But one thing is clear: in 1947, nobody would have thought to write a book about the poetry of the Pacific Northwest. T.S. Eliot's London may have been an apt symbol for our century's urban wasteland, but the city also contained an atmosphere conducive to the writing of modernist poetry. In 1947 Seattle must have looked like a poetic wasteland, an unlikely place for the forty-year-old Roethke to make good on the promises of his early career. Of the extraordinary poems in *The Lost Son* (1948), none represented more of a breakthrough than "Cuttings (later)," a poem that simultaneously harked back to his boyhood in Saginaw, Michigan, and to the greenhouse his father tended there, and, at the same time, spoke to the poet coming to full power amidst the green lushness of the Pacific Northwest, teaching his classes at the university in a room that, once again in his life, looked out on a greenhouse:

Cuttings

(later)

This urge, wrestle, resurrection of dry sticks,
Cut stems struggling to put down feet,
What saint strained so much,
Rose on such lopped limbs to a new life?

I can hear, underground, that sucking and sobbing,
In my veins, in my bones I feel it—
The small waters seeping upwards,
The tight grains parting at last.
When sprouts break out,
Slippery as a fish
I quail, lean to beginnings, sheath-wet.[2]

To be sure, a poem this good, this archetypally powerful, carries an influence that arcs well beyond the Pacific Northwest. I would argue, nonetheless, that many poets in the Northwest discovered in Roethke's work the terms for transmogrifying their landscape into language, in much the same way that a generation of southern writers discovered "the South" by reading William Faulkner's *Absalom, Absalom!* or that a generation of American-Jewish writers discovered "the City" by reading Saul Bellow's *The Adventures of Augie March.*

More than three decades have passed since Theodore Roethke blazed his poetic trail northward. Seattle has grown into one of America's chic, attractive cities; and the University of Washington's English Department no longer has to apologize for provincialism. All sorts of serious, practicing poets are happy to spend a semester, or many semesters, there.

There are other indicators of change as well: Edward Field's *A Geography of Poets* (New York: Bantam Books, 1979) included nineteen poets in a section devoted to "The Northwest"; the region has more than its fair share of "little magazines," poetry readings, and university-sponsored Writing Programs; and it has produced, thus far, three poets of undeniably major stature—William Stafford, Richard Hugo, and David Wagoner.

And yet it would be sentimental and simplistic, falsifying and plain unfair, to credit Roethke as the guiding spirit behind every line of poetry written north of San Francisco or west of Chicago. This is especially true when statements about general indebtedness ("Roethke's Impact on _____") become discussions of Roethke's "influence." Poets who are still quick to acknowledge the former find themselves increasingly uncomfortable with the latter. Roethke would, no doubt, have found this a wryly amusing turn of events. Nothing dogged his heels more than the persistent charge that he was an "imitative poet," one who had lifted his rhythms and many of his thematic concerns from William Butler Yeats. Critics glossed Roethke's claim that "I take this cadence from a man named Yeats" (from "The Dancer") far too literally.[3] For one thing, the poem's next line insists that "I take it, and I give it back again," but, more important, Roethke put whatever he learned from Yeats, and a host of others, to good purpose—namely, to give the "influences" back in poems that are as fiercely American as they are fiercely personal.

Roethke wrote nonfiction with the same precision, the same loving care about language, that went into his poetry. And one suspects that he wrote his justly famous essay "How to Write Like Somebody Else" with a double measure of his undivided attention. He wished, after all, to defend his own work and to clear the air about the vexing matter of influence. At one point in the essay he says this:

. . . Let us say that some people—often inarticulate simple types—can hear a poem, can recognize the real thing; far fewer know what a line is; and fewer yet, I suspect, are equipped to determine finally whether a writer has achieved his own tone, or whether he has been unduly influenced by another; for such a judgment involves a truly intimate knowledge not only of the particular writers concerned, but also the whole tradition of the language; a very exact medium sense; and a delicate and perceptive ear. I suggest that the central critical problem remains: whether a real poem has been created. If it has, the matter of influence becomes irrelevant. . . .

In a shrewd justification of the referential poem, or less charitably, the poem which is an anthology of other men's effects, Eliot said, "Bad poets imitate; good poets steal." In other words, take what you will with authority and see that you give it another, or even better life in the new context.[4]

Roethke is worth citing at length because his career made good on his pronouncements—that is, he grabbed with authority, listened hard, and put the result into a new context. For Roethke, talk about influence was both vague and beside the point. The real issue was the *ear,* however perplexing, however subjective, however vague it might seem as a critical measuring rod.

Roethke, of course, did not have the last word about influence. Given the nature of reviewers and critics, how could he? The term is still used, and misused, but now it is applied to *Roethke's* influence on poets like David Wagoner, Richard Hugo and, to a lesser extent, William Stafford. It is an irony that Roethke would, no doubt, have found amusing. After all, he became a Major Poet the hard way, by crawling out from beneath Yeats's shadow. His students (including Wagoner, Hugo, and James Wright) were evidently fated to do much the same thing. History refuses to repeat itself in easily identifiable ways, so there are always enough alterations and curve balls to insure a large, stable number of those doomed to repeat the mistakes of the past because they did not learn what history had to teach. Literary critics comprise a goodly portion of the community, as Roethke's "disciples" discovered when they launched into their own careers.

Nelson Bentley, an indefatigable supporter of poetry who has taught for many years at the University of Washington, likes to quip that "Northwest poetry" is characterized by its loving attention to fog, slugs, and moss. No doubt some scholar with a personal computer and a bent for statistics will prove him right, but there is more to Bentley's savvy remark than an interest in quantification. Like Faulkner, the Northwest poets write about what they know, what comes with the territory. For Faulkner, it was the "postage stamp of native soil" he called Yoknapatawpha County; for the Northwest poets, it is, indeed, often fog, slugs, and moss. But in the best Northwest poets it is more than that, as Faulkner's South was more than his neighbors in Oxford, Mississippi, usually imagined. How this happens remains a mystery we can only guess about. But the result of the process—in this case, the poetry of William Stafford, Richard Hugo, and David Wagoner—is the stuff of which studies, like the one to follow, are made. Each has become—in his own idiom, his own voice, and his own right—a major American poet; and each has published a volume of collected verse that stands as indisputable evidence that the Pacific Northwest has an enduring place in the complicated "geography" of American poetry. In large measure, it is these books, easily accessible and seminally important, that I shall explore in the next chapters.

WILLIAM STAFFORD
(c. 1984)
Photograph by Barbara Stafford

Chapter Two

William Stafford: "The Real Things We Live By"

Biographical Sketch

William Stafford was born 17 January 1914 in Hutchinson, Kansas. He grew up in a series of small Kansas towns—Wichita, Liberal, Garden City, El Dorado—as his father moved from place to place, looking for work in tough economic times.

Stafford was, however, better off than many during the Depression. He attended the University of Kansas, graduating in 1937. During World War II—from 1942 to 1946—he was a conscientious objector, serving his alternative service in camps in Arkansas, California, and Illinois. His first book, an autobiography entitled *Down in My Heart* (1947), is an account of his experience as a conscientious objector. More significant, though, may be the poems that he includes in the volume that suggest, in embryo, the poet he would become.

Stafford returned to civilian life in 1947, which, in his case, meant a return to the University of Kansas. He received his M.A. from that institution in 1946. Indeed, he would spend the bulk of his life at one academic watering hole or another. For example, from 1948 to 1950 he was an instructor in English at Lewis and Clark College in Portland, Oregon—the school that would eventually become his permanent academic base; from 1950 to 1954 he was a student assistant at the University of Iowa, where he worked toward the completion of his Ph.D. Stafford remembers his years at the University of Iowa, especially the writing seminars he both endured and enjoyed there, with mixed emotions. Remembering the experience years later, he said: "I had to learn the accomplishments and relations . . . which often alluded to publications or rivalries that were out of my ken."[1] Nonetheless, the same essay makes it clear that he liked his two years at the Iowa Workshop, and that he "served easy time" there.

Stafford was an assistant professor at Manchester College in Indiana when he received his Ph.D. in 1954. He taught there for the next academic year (the experience is reflected in his poem "Leaving a Small College") and then he moved on, this time to a position at San Jose State College in California. Once again, Stafford moved after an academic year (1955–56), but this time it was to Lewis and Clark College and a distinguished career there that spanned nearly a quarter century.

Stafford's first book of poetry, *West of Your City*, appeared in 1960, when he was forty-six-years old. But if his was a late start, at least when compared to most American poets, he made up for this in the next decade. *Traveling Through the Dark*, published in 1962, won him a National Book Award and a considerable reputation. *The Rescued Year* followed in 1966 and *Allegiances* in 1970. By the 1970s, Stafford was widely recognized as a major poet.

The 1970s made it clear that he was also among our most productive American poets. *Someday, Maybe* in 1973 was followed, in 1976, by *Braided Apart,* a collection he did with his son and fellow-poet, Kim Robert Stafford; *Smoke's Way* in 1977 was followed, in 1978, by *Writing the Australian Crawl,* a collection of Stafford's homespun, uncomplicated advice about the writing process. In an age when anxious, neurotic poets seemed to be the only sort that America produced, Stafford's easygoing, uncomplicated, and, most of all, wise reflections on his life and his craft were gusts of fresh air.

In 1980 Stafford published *Things That Happen Where There Aren't Any People,* and in that same year he retired from Lewis and Clark College. Lest one imagine, however, that the life of an emeritus professor is either placid or unproductive, one need only look at the volumes he has published recently: *Sometimes Like a Legend* (1981); *A Glass Face in the Rain* (1982), and a fascinating collaboration with the young Iowa poet, Marvin Bell, entitled *Segues: A Correspondence in Poetry* (1983).

Themes and Techniques

William Stafford's poetry has always exhibited a strong attachment to what, in "Allegiances," he calls "the real things / we live by." His language is plain, his diction flat. The result is a poetry fashioned of the elemental, by the elemental, and for the elemental. It is a poetry that dares the edges of prose, that so approximates normal speech

rhythms that, at Stafford's poetry readings, the audience is often unsure where his introductory remarks end and his poems begin.

In "Allegiances" Stafford identifies himself neither with the heroes
(who may, in fact, be homeless), nor with the "insane wind" that
"whines its strange beliefs at the traveler's ears," but rather, with the
common folk, those ordinary beings who ". . . can cling to the earth
and love / where we are, sturdy for common things."[2] That much
said, however, let me hasten to add that "Allegiances" is not a manifesto poem in the manner of, say, Archibald MacLeish's "Ars Poetica"
or Louis Simpson's "American Poetry." For one thing, Stafford is less
self-conscious—particularly about formal matters—than modernist,
and now post-modernist, poets tend to be. He prefers to remain tentative, open to whatever experiences might happen or whatever poetic
inclinations might overwhelm him. As David Wagoner put it to me:
"The Muse has been mighty good to Bill," and reading the best of
Stafford's poems, we are prone to agree. He is exactly the kind of poet
who can make talk about the muse respectable once again. For him,
poetry is a way of coming to terms with the world's strangeness and
wonder, its wisdom and its truth. Strong voices, shrill with conviction, make Stafford uncomfortable. By contrast, he gently insists on
titles that announce the tentativeness in advance: *Someday, Maybe*
(1973) or *Stories That Could Be True* (1980). He does not make poems
by grafting a literary tradition (great or otherwise) onto quotidian reality. Even more unfashionably, he does not seem to have a "program." In short, Stafford does not—indeed, he probably could not—
pack his assumptions about poetry into a single poem. Instead, they
are scattered throughout his work. He dispenses homespun wisdoms
generously, and without embarrassment.

All of which is to suggest that there are surely other candidates
with as much claim for being the poem at the center of Stafford's vision, his method, as "Allegiances." Nonetheless, that poem is a good
place to begin—and as Stafford himself might put it, you've got to
start somewhere. Let me do just that by citing the full text:

Allegiances

It is time for all the heroes to go home
if they have any, time for all of us common ones
to locate ourselves by the real things
we live by.

Far to the north, or indeed in any direction,
strange mountains and creatures have always lurked—
elves, gobblins, trolls, and spiders:—we
encounter them in dread and wonder,

But once we have tasted far streams, touched the gold,
found some limit beyond the waterfall,
a season changes, and we come back, changed
but safe, quiet, grateful.

Suppose an insane wind holds all the hills
while strange beliefs whine at the traveler's ears,
we ordinary beings can cling to the earth and love
where we are, sturdy for common things.

"Allegiances" is built on a series of reversals—not only those involving the archetype of the hero, but also those that speak to the conditions of the poet. Granted, these paradoxical "oppositions" often come to the same thing—as they do in a poem like Coleridge's "Kubla Khan." Nature resists the imposition of Kubla Khan's artificial order (the "pleasure dome"), but the poet-speaker (who "would build that dome in air") is able to join sun and ice into an image [god-like? Faustian?] of fearful power:

Could I revive within me
Her [i.e., the Abyssinian maid's] symphony and song,
To such delight 'twould win me,
That with music loud and long,
I would build that dome in air,
That sunny dome! those caves of ice!
And all who heard should see them there,
And all would cry, Beware! Beware!
His flashing eyes, his floating hair!
Wave a circle round him thrice,
And close your eyes with holy dread. . . .

By contrast, Stafford's speaker gets his nourishment from humbler sources, from the earth and the lives lived within its rhythms. The problem of course, is that the allegiances in Stafford's poetry are complicated. There is as much attraction as there is resistance to an "insane wind" that holds the hills and the "strange beliefs" that "whine at a traveler's ears." One doesn't have to be a Coleridgean Romantic to realize that "dread and wonder" pack a wallop that the "safe, quiet, grateful" never can. Stafford's poem qualifies both what it celebrates and what it presumably dismisses. In short, one of his allegiances is to poetry, to stanzas built from the very materials that the poem per se seems to argue against. "Change" is worth our allegiance every bit as much as realizing that mere *adventure* is not a sufficient condition for our full humanity.

At the same time Stafford is skillful enough to build tensions into lines that extoll the virtues of ordinary life plainly lived. At the point where his language turns flat, purposefully *un*exotic, the speaker talks about those who "can cling to the earth and love / where we are. . . ." The line break suggests the possibility of "love" both as a noun (as in line 15) or a verb (as in lines 15–16). The implied metaphor throughout the poem pits those in motion (always questing, moving beyond the next hill to the next, far stream) against those in stasis, rooted in the soil, "sturdy for common things"—in a word, *plantlike*. It is the "insane wind" that bends (and possibly breaks) those who travel, who leave the security of home. "Ordinary beings," on the other hand, "cling to the earth" and are presumably stronger for that commitment.

Stafford's tone is another matter. By reversing the usual expectations of the quest and the literary productions it has engendered, he apparently throws his lot with simpler souls. But like Robert Frost (who also seems to speak for, and to champion, the cause of earthly wisdom), the home-and-hearth dimension of Stafford's poetry can be deceptive. Both poets regularly entertain darker visions than common readers generally acknowledge. This is not to argue for a "dark Stafford" in the ways that a biographer like Lawrance Thompson argues for a "dark Frost." Indeed, no two poets strike us as being more unlike in temperament. Frost lugged a nasty streak through the underside of his poems, and an even wider one through his personal life. With Stafford, the "darkness"—or perhaps a better term might be the *radical subversiveness*—lies just beneath or behind or above the calm surface of his poems. I leave speculation about Stafford's life—his placid exterior, his unflappable goodwill, his pacifism, his religious convictions, his political leanings—to others. Wonder brings him to his poems, and it is there that he has said God's plenty about the light and darkness of our condition, and about the constant amazement and tentative truths we all share. "Allegiances" is, in this sense, a good place to begin a reassessment of one of our wiser, more important, contemporary American poets.

William Stafford published his first collection of poetry, *West of Your City* in 1960. He was forty-six years old. Not since Wallace Stevens (who delayed the publication of his first collection, *Harmonium,* until he was fifty years old) has a major American poet had such a late start. Generally speaking, both the excitements and the indignities of being a "young poet" are part of one's initiation into the world of highbrow poetry. As legend would have it, Theodore Roethke stormed into a classroom at the University of Washington on his fiftieth birthday and announced, half playfully, half in genuine indignation: "Now maybe those guys [i.e., the reviewers] will quit calling me a 'young poet.' " A poet in America is young right up to the day he or she collects a check from Social Security.

By contrast, Stafford seemingly arrived full-blown, with a recognizable voice and a firm sense of congenial material. Granted, his voice developed, was surer in some poems than others, and much the same things could be said about his ever-widening range of subject matter (including landscapes and experiences associated with the Pacific Northwest), but Stafford's career, in toto, makes a powerful argument on behalf of patience. From the beginning he struck an easy accommodation to the vagaries of being a poet in America.

Stafford writes about his childhood and early schooling with an uncomplicated affection that is likely to convince even the most hardened skeptic. His account of those years insists on the value of experiences other than ones filled with oedipal conflict, nightmare, deprivation, and angst. Early on, his "allegiance"—his sense of where genuine poems come from—has been to common, sturdy things:

We moved from one little town to another during my school years, following my father's jobs, which varied, but always provided income for our needs and books. We liked the towns and countryside, which we fished, hunted, and camped along the mild, wandering streams. Our lives were quiet and the land was very steady.[3]

When Stafford reminisces in prose, his tone is heavy with the pastoral and the nostalgic, but his poems often suggest otherwise. Here, for example, are representative lines from "Some Shadows" that disturb and complicate in ways not easy to square with his insistences about quiet lives and steady lands:

> . . . Later, though she was frightened,
> She loved, like anyone.
> A lean man, a cruel, took her.
> I am his son.
>
> He was called Hawk by the town people . . .
> Forgive me these shadows I cling to, good people,
> Trying to hold quiet in my prologue.
> Hawks cling the barrens wherever I live.
> The world says "Dog eat dog"
>
> (112)

When Stafford gives public readings of this presumably "confessional" poem—all the more disturbing, I think, because its strong rhymes and *abcb* stanzas are as elemental as they are ominous—he usually follows it with a deflating anecdote:

Shortly after this poem appeared in a magazine [Stafford begins]—a little magazine it was—a neighbor hurried over to sister Peg's house and said: "Gee, Peggy, I didn't know your father was such a mean man. Look here at what Bill wrote." Well, Peg read the poem and then laughed and said: "Oh, that's just Bill *romancing* again!"[4]

Sister Peg is, of course, partly right: their father was neither a man named Hawk, nor was he the lean, cruel man described in the poem. Indeed, one would hardly need to be a specialist of Stafford's poetry to find counterexamples filled with "good fathers" ("In Medias Res," "Vocation," "Father's Voice"). Very often the speaker in a Stafford poem tries desperately to reconnect himself with parental figures, the old farm house—as in "The Farm on the Great Plains." But Sister Peg simplifies too much, dismisses too quickly. Poems may well be romances or fictions or lies—whichever terms you prefer—but they are also *supreme* fictions, to borrow Wallace Stevens's canny phrase. If the "details" are biographically inaccurate, it does not follow as the night the day that the poem is less humanly true.

"Shadows" still cling to the speaker in "Some Shadows" and they raise serious questions about the tone of the last stanza's address to the "good people." After all, this is a world that loudly declares what it imagaines to be an unassailable truth—namely, "dog eat dog." By contrast, the speaker declares his humanity softly, in the whispers, the "prologue," that is the poem. "Hawks"—whether his father or predatory birds—"cling the barrens" where all of us, the speaker and others, have a stake in clinging, in holding on.

Put another way, the grip of the past is so strong in Stafford's imagination that he has no need for the artificial mythic histories celebrated in *The Waste Land*. This may partially explain his resistances to T. S. Eliot. More is at stake here than bookishness or the vexing business of "influence." For Stafford, vestiges of the past cannot *not* be noted; moreover, they must be noted with a particular style. They are the stuff of which many of his poems are made. And the result is not, I would submit, the same thing as Stafford himself insisting that his childhood was idyllic or that "Not till I finished my BA degree at the University of Kansas [in 1937] . . . did I ever see an adult drunk or enraged or seriously menacing."[5] In a sense, both "A Statement on Life and Writings" and "Some Shadows" are true, but only the one that begins "You would not want too reserved a speaker— / that is a cold way to live" is a poem. More to the biographical point, it is a poem that only becomes possible when one has "withdrawn" from such a world, and from those who ask your sister if "Some Shadows" is an accurate description of Earl Ingersoll Stafford. In Stafford's wonderful phrase (from "Lit Instructor") Right "has a long and intricate name" and whether one is teaching a poem or writing it (Stafford's pun, I suspect, is intentional), the "saying of it is a lonely thing."

In "Bi-Focal" this split vision is precisely the poem's point. There is a love that "is of the earth only," and the "fixed, inexorable" legend lying underneath. With the right bifocals one can see them simultaneously and, I would add, necessarily because:

> . . . the world happens twice—
> once what we see it as;
> second it legends itself
> deep, the way it is.
>
> (48)

Turning "legend" into a verb (normally, something one doesn't applaud) makes all the difference here; the world not only has properties (what we *see*), but the ability to "legend" itself into something deeper and, significantly enough, "darker" than the love that exists on surfaces. Granted, the legend that is beginning to move is hardly that "rough beast" Yeats envisioned in "The Second Coming," but certainly Stafford's poetry aims at this second mode of *seeing,* however much he attends to the surfaces of love and however much he celebrates them. It is his doubleness of vision, its bifurcated (or bifocaled, if you will) qualities, that interests me. Stafford can be didactic, even preachy, but always with a light, tricky touch. Here, for example, are the opening lines of "Freedom," a title with enough quicksand in it to sink even a good poet:

> Freedom is not following a river.
> Freedom is following a river,
>   though, if you want to . . .
> It is knowing that luck makes a difference.
>   (239)

What looks like a poem bristling with national virtue turns out, in fact, to be about artistic freedom and, more particularly, about William Stafford's modus operandi:

> If you are oppressed, wake up about
> four in the morning; most places,
> you can usually be free some of the time
>   if you wake up before other people.
>   (239)

And that, of course, turns out to be true, not only for this poem, but for many of the poems he wrote from *West of Your City* onward. Critics—even those who prefer to work late at night rather than early in the morning—can share one thing with Stafford; we, too, know that "luck makes a difference."

Although Stafford published *Down in My Heart* (1947), a nonfictional account, punctuated with some poetry, of his wartime experiences as a conscientious objector, his career as a poet begins with his first major volume, *West of Your City.* He had joined Lewis and Clark's English Department in 1948 and, with the exception of visiting stints, he has been associated with that Portland, Oregon, liberal arts institution throughout his career. *West of Your City* is divided— significantly, I think—into three sections: "Midwest," "Far West," and "Outside," The "Midwest" section (containing ten poems) incorporates the collection's title as an epigraph that reverberates westward: "West of your city into the fern / *sympathy, sympathy rolls the train* . . ." In America, west is the direction of promise, that place where, Stafford [ambivalently?] argues, "corn still lies." But west is also a landscape in which *all* the possibilities of "leaves"—as parts of a plant, as the act of departure, as the pages of a book—exist simultaneously:

> Cocked in that land tactile as leaves
> wild things wait crouched in those valleys
> west of your city outside your lives
> in the ultimate wind, the whole land's wave.
> Come west and see; touch these leaves.
>
>   (29)

In short, "West of Your City" is a playful epigram. One cannot read the book without making good on Stafford's urgings to "touch these leaves." On the other hand, however, the "wild things [that] wait crouched in those valleys" may include the panting lizard of "At the Bomb Testing Site" who grips its elbows hard against the desert floor, "ready for a change." There are unities in *West of Your City* that are much subtler than the book's strong directional arrows account for.

"Ceremony" is a representative poem, not only because it nearly convinces us that Nature has a symbolic dimension (in this case, muskrats with enough savvy and literary good sense to bite the speaker on the "third finger of my left hand" and thus wed this human intruder with larger rhythms), but also because it is a fair accounting of how vision and poetic technique combine in Stafford's best poetry. "Ceremony" both pulls toward, and away from, literary form/literary content. Its thirteen lines (three quatrains, albeit unrhymed, and a half-couplet) tease us into memories of the sonnet:

Ceremony

> On the third finger of my left hand
> under the bank of the Ninnescah
> a muskrat whirled and bit to the bone.
> The mangled hand made the water red.
>
> That was something the ocean would remember:
> I saw me in the current flowing through the land

rolling, touching roots, the world incarnadined,
and the river richer by a kind of marriage.

While in the woods an owl started quavering
with drops like tears I raised my arm.
Under the bank a muskrat was trembling
with meaning my hand would wear forever.

In that river my blood flowed on.

(30)

In an intriguing comparative study entitled "The Bite of the Musk-rat: Judging Contemporary Poetry" David Young argues that the self-effacing qualities of "Ceremony" are much superior to the "swollen ego" of James Dickey's "The Poisoned Man." What Young's reading comes to is the suspicion that Dickey's poem is too self-consciously mythic, too *literary*. By contrast, Stafford (despite a jarring, erudite word like "incarnadined") convinces us that the poem actually happened, as reported, on the banks of the Ninnescah, rather than being "made up" in the library stacks. Moreover, Stafford's hand bears out Young's suspicions; the scar speaks volumes about how his poems originate. But that said, what about the second stanza's large claims? Is the muskrat bite and the resulting blood "something the ocean would remember," or is Stafford merely gilding the poetic lily, committing that New Critical sin we used to call the pathetic fallacy? Does Stafford's speaker *really* imagine himself—that is to say, his blood—"flowing through the land" and, thereby, incarnadining [i.e., coloring it crimson red] the river both by word and marriage? As often happens in Stafford's poetry, our answer can only be tentative, an uneasy combination of "yes" and "no." Things happen to us in the world that are surprising—a muskrat bites down on somebody's ring finger, for example—and, unsurprisingly, we give significance to such moments. That, I take it, is what the second stanza is about, and why "the word incarnadined" is such an important phrase. Language is as much a part of the "ceremony" as is Nature.

But the poem does not stop with line 8, although many another poet would have been content with the resonances of "the river made richer by a kind of marriage." Leaving aside the qualifying tone of "a kind of" (poets out for the strongest possible exit would, no doubt, cut the seemingly extraneous words and get from "richer" to marriage

much more quickly), the third stanza sets up the necessary precondi-
tions that make line 13 ("In that river my blood flowed on") both
forceful and poetically "right." Part of the third stanza's ambivalence
generates from the punctuation that is conspicuous by its absence.
Should there, for example, be a comma after "woods" and a full stop
after "quavering"? Or does the owl quaver "with drops like tears"?
In short, what *is* the relation between the -ing verbs associated with
animals and and the "meaning" the speaker's hand "would wear forever"? Does the speaker raise his arm in anger? in supplication?
in reverence? in awe? Perhaps such moments are, by definition,
ephemeral, only captured in that "recollection" Wordsworth talks
about in his "Preface" to the *Lyrical Ballads.* One thing, however, is
clear: the poem's final line moves outward (a point Young also
stresses), away from narrowly confessional concerns, and into the
world. We read the "my blood" of line 13 very differently from the
"my left hand" of line 1.

"Ceremony" illustrates Stafford's strong commitment to process, to
exploration, to moving outward in gestures that "embrace" experience
rather than border it by artificial constructions. In a recent interview
he put it this way: ". . . it's important to let the process of writing
bring about things rather than be just the writing down of things
that are already brought about,"[6] and versions of this fundamental
posture have dotted Stafford's prose since the mid-sixties. *West of Your
City* was an early, poetic demonstration. Stafford seems so "natural"
a poet (one who speaks with an unaffected honesty and a wisdom an-
chored in what often travels under the name Real Life) that we are
surprised by the hard work, the scratchings out, the revisions, and
the heaps of "rejection" that were also part of the scenario.

For Stafford, the Midwest is as much condition as place ("Mine was
a Midwest home—['One Home' begins] you can keep your world"),
but one not easily subsumed under the warm tent of nostalgia.
Granted, the fathers of these poems teach wise, important lessons,
but they must be applied in the wider orbits of leave-taking. In "Circle of Breath," for example, the speaker drives in from the West on
the night his father dies and stands, a "truant from knowing," as
dark shadows sweep through the room. Returns have as many sharp
edges, produce as much ambivalence, as leave-taking. Lines 5–10
move backward in time to a preparatory lesson, a cautionary tale
about the life each of us lives:

> [Once] we parked the car in a storm and walked into a field
> to know how it was to be cut off, out in the dark alone.
> My father and I stood together while the storm went by.
>
> A windmill was there in the field giving its little cry
> while we stood calm in ourselves, knowing we could go home.
>
> (32)

Stafford's second book deepens his investigation of *Traveling Through the Dark* (more often as father than son), but the curious blending of unflinching honesty and muted rebellion continues. The collection won Stafford a National Book Award, and the voice that had made a brilliant debut two years earlier became an American fact. The title poem "Traveling Through the Dark" is simultaneously a narrative and a condition, a tale about what a speaker did after encountering a dead deer "on the edge of the Wilson River road" and the moral ambivalences each of us faces in the dark quotidian we travel through. Stafford's characteristically understated intensities were never stronger, never more compelling. The first two stanzas set the situation in a matter of fact, almost clinically detached way. Along country roads dead deer are a fact of contemporary life: "It is usually best to roll them into the canyon; / that road is narrow; to swerve might make more dead" (61).

The poem pivots on the word "swerve"—as a physical condition and as a psychological fact. If Stafford were a poet given to public utterance, he might have launched into a hectoring denunciation of the automobile and, thus, placed himself on the side of those angels who weep whenever Man inflicts himself on Nature. After all, the deer in question was hardly struck down by old age; rather, it was hit by an earlier automobile, no doubt one also "traveling through the dark." Leaving the carcass on the road only compounds the problems by making "more dead." Hence, the folk wisdom we know in such cases—without "thinking," without ambivalence—is to roll the dead animal into the canyon, out of harm's way.

The rub—and one that Stafford builds by fleshing in the details of the story while, at the same time, holding back certain information— is that this deer is pregnant. Suddenly the moral question becomes as complicated as the implications rippling outward. Moreover, the speaker cannot *not* "hesitate." He is the one who *sees* ("By the glow of the tail-light"), but he is also the one who must ultimately *act*. The others of his group remain in the car which, significantly enough, aims its lowered parking lights ahead and keeps its "steady engine" purring. The three principals, then, are the deer, the speaker, and the automobile—and they conflate into an image of the speaker standing "in the glare of the exhaust turning red" (the speaker? the exhaust? both?).

In a manuscript version of the poem (dated June 1956) line 16 reads: "All around I could hear the wilderness listen." The first two words have been changed to "Around our group . . ." The difference is crucial, not only because "All around" is an incorrect idiom, but, more important, because it is imprecise. The "group" here has something of the same impact on the wilderness as Wallace Stevens's poem about the jar placed in Tennessee. Both define the landscape, the situation, in a new way.

The final couplet resolves that new situation. The speaker, thinking hard for everyone—as the Representative Man, the Poet—pushes the deer over the edge. Generally speaking, prepositional phrases smack of a romantic lilt that most contemporary poets work hard to avoid. Metrically, it is a function of the anapest, but a line from Yeats's "The White Birds" might make the point more dramatically: "I would that we were, my beloved, white birds / on the foam / of the tide." I've scanned the line to make the metrics of the two back-to-back prepositional phrases clearer. "Traveling Through the Dark" also ends with a double anapest, but to a markedly different effect. The motion stands in opposition to *swerving*—suggesting finality, as the deer tumbles down the canyonside—but it also makes clear that swerving of this sort (rather than the swerving that missed the dead deer in the first place) is at the heart of Stafford's poem. In the largest sense I suppose all of us "travel through the dark," unsure of our destination or what we might stumble across along the way. Stafford's very title teases us into speculations of this generalized, philosophical sort, but it is also important to remember that a poem grounds itself in specifics. That is precisely what he has done as he thinks hard for all of us in a "swerving" each reader can vicariously share.

"Thinking for Berky" operates on similar principles. It, too, is a poem built around a participle, although, there, the speaker seems to be the only one *thinking* about Berky. In the late night sirens speak of emergencies, of some bad end that is Berky's lot. Roused from sleep, the speaker rescues her from memory by telling her story. In this sense he thinks for Berky as well as about her, articulating what she can only feel.

Berky's saga is the stuff of melodrama, of "ambulance or the patrol," of violence, but, in the poem, transmogrified into a species of tragedy. Granted, all the recognitions, the catharsis, the tragic insight reside in the speaker. In short, the poem is an act of identification as well as an exorcism, a vehicle for aligning oneself with the outsider rather than with those "survivors" who cling to their safety and their beds, "so far and good."

Berky's past is sketched in quick strokes, more outline than developed narrative, but the essential elements that formed her psyche are there nonetheless:

> The wildest of all, her father and mother cruel,
> farming out there beyond the old stone quarry
> where highschool lovers parked their lurching cars,
> Berky learned to love in that dark school.
>
> (64)

The sheer starkness of the elemental language (e.g., "wildest," "cruel") is so understated, so basic, that readers willingly fill in the gaps. After all, this is a familiar, oft-told tale. My hunch is that, for Stafford, Berky is a composite rather than a biographical figure from this past; for us, she is an archetype and, in the poem, it is this attribute that matters.

More important, however, is the quiet, even sly way that Stafford wrinkles in verbal complexities without tipping his hand or spoiling the broad outlines of his narrative. Berky is, indeed, the outsider, the one alienated from the larger community. But the quarry (beyond which her "cruel" parents farm, on land that because of its proximity to the stone quarry, must be "cruel" as well) is also an apt description of Berky herself. The sirens will "hunt [her] down"; she is the *quarry* that the "stone quarry" produced. Stafford wrote this poem in January 1955. Four years later Robert Lowell would describe a lovers' lane using very similar imagery:

> One dark night
> my Tudor Ford climbed the hill's skull;
> I watched for love-cars. Lights turned down,
> they lay together, hull to hull,

> where the graveyard shelves on the town . . .
> My mind's not right.[7]

There are, of course, important differences. Lowell uses the "love-cars" as an index of his own aloneness, and as a way of creeping up on the starkly confessional "My mind's not right." By contrast, Stafford eschews this sort of biographical candor; he conceals as much as he reveals, preferring the oblique angle to the shot between a reader's eyes. For all the metaphysical dazzle of Lowell's love-cars lying "hull to hull," the meaning is explicit and one-dimensional. In Berky's case, however, she "learned to love in that dark school." Granted, it is a terrible love, born from bad circumstances and desperation, but something deeper, and richer, than a physical act is involved here.

Indeed, Stafford's next stanza makes the doubleness of love clear:

> Early her face was turned away from home
> toward any hardworking place; but still her soul
> with terrible things to do, was alive, looking out
> for the rescue that—surely, some day—would have to come.
>
> (64)

These lines are packed with favorite Stafford idioms (e.g., "rescue," "some day") and they give Berky's story its aspects of romance and, then, tragedy. What remains incorruptible is her soul; what remains firmly fixed—at least in the speaker's imagination—is Berky's destiny. What must be cannot be, what cannot be must be; this is the tragic condition, as applicable to an Oedipus and a Lear as it is to less rarefied beings like Berky.

Ironically, her "rescue" comes not from father-teacher-fireman-cop (those forces of the super-ego who wear official uniforms and represent Society with a capital letter), but, rather, from the poet whose poem "rescues" her life from misunderstanding and anonymity. The key terms, I think, are magic and mystery, and they apply equally to Berky and to the poem written about her:

> Windiest nights, Berky, I have thought for you,
> and no matter how lucky I've been I've touched wood.
> There are things not solved in our town though tomorrow came:
> there are things time passing can never make come true.
>
> (64)

Berky's romanticism, her need to believe that a change "—surely some day—would have to come" is linked to the good townspeople who believe that unsolved things will be remedied by morning and that "time passing" can make passive dreams "come true." Both parties are wrong, but it is Berky who tests out her thesis in the world's "dark school," in the night where an alive soul seeks out its destiny.

When Stafford first began publishing, he had regular encounters with those disappointments and indignities that afflict most contemporary poets. Indeed, the essays in *Writing the Australian Crawl* are filled with eloquent defenses of Stafford's aesthetic, his refusal to be molded by fashion or hamstrung by the programmatic. Unlike Robert Lowell (who once complained that when he first started writing poetry, he couldn't get anything "accepted," but very shortly, he couldn't get anything rejected—and that, ironically enough, the latter condition was much worse, much more anxious than the former), Stafford continues to cherish his low batting average with the journals. *Harper's,* for example, wanted him to improve the last lines of "Thinking for Berky," a fact he carefully noted on a typed version of the poem. *The Ladies Home Journal* "liked" the poem, but did not take it. Meanwhile, Stafford tinkered with the concluding stanza. Here is an early version:

> We live in an occupied country, misunderstood;
> freedom will come after millions of intricate moves.
> Sirens will hunt down Berky from the quiet of our beds
> while in the night we lie, so far and good.

In the published version the political (or possibly, sociopolitical) shadings of the first line remain (Stafford's assertion that *we* are the occupiers of our "occupied country" at the same time that we must, inevitably, share our space with mystery and magic), but the bulk of the stanza has been changed:

> Justice will take us millions of intricate moves.
> Sirens will hunt down Berky, you survivors in your beds
> listening through the night, so far and good.
>
> (65)

"Justice" is more apt where collectives are concerned. In a later poem entitled "Freedom," Stafford pitches the argument ("Freedom is not following a river. / Freedom is following a river, / though, if you want to") as a matter of individual choice.

But what of the slumbering "survivors"? Earlier I talked about
Stafford's radical subversiveness; the sardonic tone of "so far and
good" is yet another example of this phenomenon. What begins as
matter-of-fact, even unpoetic, narrative ends in poetry of a purer sort.
The comma after "night" separates the phrase "so far and good" from
its possible antecedents. The referent is ambiguous (is it to "you survivors" or to "night"?), at the same time it is hauntingly accurate.
After all, survivors have, by definition, survived; they don't bother to
knock on wood or to speculate about the likes of a Berky. For them,
justice makes its intricate moves and things not solved today will be
settled tomorrow. Stafford knows better, and that knowledge is what
"Thinking for Berky" is about.

Stafford addresses the problem more directly in "With my Crowbar
Key," a poem about the writing of poetry. As Jonathan Holden
points out: "Poetry can help define the shape of sloughed processes."[8]
Stafford puts the paradox this way:

> I do tricks in order to know:
> careless I dance,
> then turn to see
> the mark to turn God left for me.
>   (65)

His essays are filled with teasing indications that exploration makes
for better poetry than journeys with set goals (or what Stafford likes
to call "programs"), that "careless" dancing is closer to the American
grain than the intricate patterning of, say, a Morris dance. Only
when one looks back can God's mark be seen; retrospection, rather
than frontal vision, is the crowbar key that unlocks the world's mysteries—and makes poetry possible.

Traveling Through the Dark is divided into three sections. Curiously
enough, the first is "In Medias Res," a title full of classical echoes
and hints that the book will be "in the middle of things." Stafford's
poem "In Medias Res" begins on what looks for all the world like
Main Street in a typical Stafford town: Father walks ahead "in
shadow" and the speaker's son following "behind coming into the
streetlight." But that said, certain words resonate beyond, or behind,
the contemporary narrative structure (e.g., "one-stride god,"
"shield," "shades"). In the concluding couplet Stafford "pulls the
string," makes the oblique references of the previous twelve lines

clear: " 'Aneas!' I cried, 'just man, defender!' / And our town [Troy] burned and burned" (62). Granted, "in Medias Res" is not a traditional sonnet in the manner of Yeats's "Leda and the Swan," but it seems loosely modeled on that great poem. Stafford retains the fourteen-line unit and something of the central spirit in Yeats's poem; what he relinquishes—no small matters—are the other formal elements of the sonnet: metrical regularity and a recognizable rhyme scheme.

Stafford tends to be evasive—or, perhaps, merely tricky—when it comes to the organizational principles that go into the making of a book. As he puts it:

. . . I try to keep poems that are near each other from detracting. Partly it's a negative consideration: Be sure not to have a sequence in which one poem might sabotage another or create some unintentionally ludicrous effect. I'm always scared about that.[9]

That much said, "Parentage"—a poem that follows "In Medias Res" from the discreet distance of six intervening poems—provides yet another view of the father looking over his shoulder (or vice versa) at his son:

> My father didn't really belong in history.
> He kept looking over his shoulder at some mistake.
> He was a stranger to me, for I belong.
>
> (67)

In this case, "belong" has the smack of passivity, of acceptance: "I'd just as soon be pushed by events to where I belong." Nothing could be more straightforward ("[I] want to have the right amount of fear, / preferring to be saved and not, like him, heroic.") and, at the same time, more dependent on its elusive quality of tone. Is the speaker being "serious" here? Or, if one drops the New Critical strictures against biographical interpretation, is this Stafford, the conscientious objector during World War II and a lifelong disciple of passive resistance, holding forth? At a reading a few years ago Stafford seized on Thomas Mann's quip that "A hero is a national calamity," and in his "down-home" and sly way he made the audience think about herohood in new ways. "Parentage" is one of those ways. "Right"—as the speaker of "Lit Instructor" knows—has "a long and complicated name." One could say the same thing about a word like "hero."

So many of Stafford's poems have a casual, dashed-off look that the string of plain assertions in "Passing Remark" strike us as exactly the right harmony of manifesto and man. Granted, the "confessions" that the poem announces are not likely to rival those of Robert Lowell or Anne Sexton or W. D. Snodgrass or Sylvia Plath, but that, of course, is part of Stafford's playful point. His poems give more space to strategies of exploration than to lamentations of regret; his personae know more about the forest than the loony bin, more about continuity than breakdown, more about love than narcissism. Rather than making much ado about nothing, Stafford tends to make little ado about everything. In "Passing Remark" (*The Rescued Year,* 131) he presents— self-consciously, I think—a portrait of the artist that the more flamboyant of our confessional poets have nearly obliterated:

> In scenery I like flat country.
> In life I don't like much to happen.
>
> In personalities I like mild colorless people.
> And in colors I prefer gray and brown.
>
> My wife, a vivid girl from the mountains,
> says, "Then why did you choose me?"
>
> Mildly I lower my brown eyes—
> there are so many things admirable people do not
>   understand.

This is not, I would submit, merely a case of opposites attracting, but, rather, a testament to those reservoirs of the interior that remain hidden. It is, if you will, a part of what makes Stafford's work so radically subversive, his tone so perplexing and difficult. If, for example, it is true that "mildly" is precisely the word to describe how his speaker might "lower" his eyes, it is also true that "admirable people" misunderstand him. How could they not? If the evidence is stacked on the side of flat landscapes, bland colors, and non-action, why, then, *choose* a "vivid girl from the mountains"?

If, however, one begins to realize that in poetry, as in life, the whole is *more* than the sum of its parts, that love is as much a mysterious condition as it is a set of facts that jibe, then one can see this vivid, mountain wife as an instance of the "many things" that even "admirable people do not understand." Stafford's speaker is vulnerable to the charge of arrogance, of superiority—after all, he presumably knows better than his commonsensical wife—but the real culprit here is "understanding." Like *wisdom* (another loaded term Stafford views with wry suspicion), "understanding" often has a habit of missing the essential point.

And since I've broken out of a chronological consideration of Stafford's work—an inevitable, but not altogether unhappy fate, given the nature of his consistency of vision and technique during the last twenty-five years—let me suggest a word or two about a curious, and often misread, Stafford poem entitled "Judgments." If "admirable people" read "Passing Remark" and still feel that, by all accounts, this flat, unexciting person should not have ended up with a vivid mountain girl, they think of "Judgments" as filled with mean-spirited accusation. It's one thing, after all, to hurl "judgments" at oneself (confessional poets have made it their stock-in-trade) and quite another to heave godlike judgments at one's peers. And isn't this, after all, what "Judgments" does? It's as if Stafford were attending, or thinking about attending, a high school reunion, and reverie calls him to Ellen, George, and Tom:

> I accuse—
>> Ellen: you have become forty years old,
>> and successful, tall, well-groomed,
>> gracias, thoughtful, a secretary.
>> Ellen, I accuse.
>
> (118)

The stanzas aimed at George and Tom retain the pattern. Like Zola, Stafford begins with *J'accuse,* but his bill of particulars is limited to a scant three lines, followed by an accusatory refrain that brings the argument full circle. Each of the protagonists ends with a snake's tail in his or her mouth; trapped inside the stanza, poetic closure creates a disquieting effect not unlike that which swept through the congregants who heard Jonathan Edwards's "Sinners in the Hands of an Angry God." "Judgments" fixes—and reduces—lives in a formulated phrase.

But, I hasten to point out, Stafford includes himself in this judgmental scenario:

> Last I accuse—
>   Myself: my terrible poise, knowing
>   even this, knowing that when we
>   sprawled in the world
>   and were ourselves part of it; now
>   we hold it firmly away with gracious
>   gestures (like this of mine!) we've achieved.
>   (119)

The uncompromising honesty Stafford directs at others turns inward with even greater accuracy. A poem like "Judgments" is not only the "gracious gesture" he acknowledges parenthetically, but evidence of the "terrible poise" with which he simultaneously empathizes and judges. There was a time, this poem wants to say, when all of us (classmates, childhood chums, the "us" at a younger, more innocent stage) "sprawled in the world / and were ourselves part of it." Now, there is distancing, whether it parades itself as smug success, the coolness of managerial skill, or the aesthetic known as irony. Each holds the world at an arm's length; each is an avatar of the accused. The difference, of course, is that Stafford *knows* he is both accuser and accused, and that is the blessing and the curse of consciousness, of being a poet. It is also the victory this poem is made of, and an index of Stafford's deceptive, even brutal, radical subversiveness.

This extended aside over, let's return to *Traveling Through the Dark*. In 1948 Stafford's "travels" took him to Portland, Oregon, and, given his interest in westward movements and the pioneer spirit, to a significantly named institution called Lewis and Clark College. "Lake Chelan" is one of his earliest—and still most impressive—efforts at capturing the essence of the northwestern landscape. To be sure, the actual Lake Chelan, as Jonathan Holden points out,[10] is in northern Washington, but that is simply to say uppercase Truth counts for more than the smaller truth of "facts":

> They call it regional, this relevance—
> the deepest place we have: in this pool forms
> the model of our land, a lonely one,

> responsive to the wind. Everything we own
> has brought us here: from here we speak.
>
> (84)

In something like the paradox Robert Frost poses in "The Gift Out-right" ("The land was ours, before we were the land's"), Stafford builds a series of equations (regional/relevance; what we won/what brings us to the lake; and, finally, the central question of all writing, language/silence) into a composite portrait of an individual lake and a universal human condition.

"Regionalism" is often a patronizing term of dismissal, a way of suggesting that one is delimited by having chosen the wrong environment. The "hot center" is, so the argument goes, somewhere else—in Brahmin Boston if one has the nineteenth-century American writer in mind or New York City for his twentieth-century counterpart. Those out to move and shake literary opinion make it their business to be "where the [publishing] action" is. And *they* are likely to prefer the familiar (read: urban) to the exotic life west of the Hudson and to turn a deaf ear to arguments about, say, the Bloomsbury crowd as more "provincial" than the provincials. They are the ones who slap the label of "regional" onto "Lake Chelan."

Granted, all serious poets try to squirm out of the cramped life one must lead under a label's thumb, but those tagged as regionalists have a special difficulty. Protest too loudly and one's argument sounds like sour grapes (e.g., "I could have made it in the Big Apple all right, but I *prefer* East Overshoe, Idaho.") Stafford writes prose in the same sotto voce that makes his poetry seem so gentle, so reasonable, so fully human. And here, too, there is method in his apparently endless stock of good-naturedness. In an issue of *Northwest Review* devoted to his work the editors have wisely included a short statement written for the occasion that Stafford calls "On Being Local." It is worth reprinting here:

All events and experiences are local, somewhere. And all human enhancements of events and experiences—all the arts—are regional in the sense that they derive from immediate relation to felt life.

It is this immediacy that distinguishes art. And paradoxically, the more local the feeling in art, the more all people can share it; for that vivid encounter with the stuff of the world is our common ground.

Artists, knowing this mutual enrichment that extends everywhere, can

act, and praise, and criticize, as insiders—the means of art is the life of all
people. And that life grows and improves by being shared. Hence, it is good
to welcome any region you live in or come to think of, for that is where life
happens to be, right where you are.[11]

"Welcome" is, indeed, the key word, characterizing not only Stafford's
open-arms approach to experience, but his philosophy of poetic com-
position. Revision, for example, is usually defined as cutting fat,
compressing imagery, reducing waste motion. Stafford brings a healthy dose of skepticism to the injunctions of Ezra Pound that one generation of poets after another has handed on like a runner's baton:

. . . I would rather be wholehearted and be welcome about anything I write.
The correct attitude to take about anything you write is "Welcome! Welcome!"[12]

Lake Chelan is, as Stafford insists, "the deepest place we have"—
not because the lake is literally deep, but because what the lake comes
to stand for represents a model of the bedrock, historical experience
out of which we came and to which, despite ourselves, we return. The
central contrast is between what is ephemeral (including the dismissal
implied in those who call it "regional") and what is "deep," between
our need to "speak" and the conditions that make speech possible and
"dumbness." "From here we speak," the speaker of the poem insists,
and that is, indeed, the point.
    The next stanza compresses history into metaphors of the frontier
experience, that restless direction toward which all of American culture psychologically moves. And it is here that Stafford deepens the
texture of paradox he announced earlier with "deepest places": "The
sun stalks among these peaks to sight / the lake down aisles, long
like a gun" (84). The line break makes both meanings of "sight" (the
act of seeing; an observation taken with a sighting instrument) operate simultaneously and, later, it contributes to the ambiguity of referent with regard to "long like a gun" (aisles? or, just as possibly,
"sun"). The stanza gradually deepens into the admixtures of "pure
poetry" that are Stafford's trademark, culminating in "the pelt of the
mountains / rinsed in the sun and that sound." The sound is the fer-
ryboat's toot, but it is more than that. Sight and sound call us to the
things of an older world, to a time when Lake Chelan stood green
and dazzling, when men looked at Nature in an awe that F. Scott
Fitzgerald captures in the concluding lines of *The Great Gatsby:*

. . . I became aware of the old island that flowered once for Dutch sailors' eyes—a fresh, green breast of the new world [and] for a transitory enchanted moment man must have held his breath in the presence of this continent, compelled into an aesthetic contemplation he neither understood nor desired, face to face for the last time in history with something commensurate to his capacity for wonder.

"Suppose" is the triggering word of the next stanza, one that suggests the continuity of "story" and the abiding power of the lake. Granted, we are given no hints as to how or why the lake might "occur" to a person far off, but confronted by some contemporary "problem,"

> he might hear a word
> so dark he drowns an instant, and stand dumb
> for the centuries of his country and suave
> hills beyond the stranger's sight.
>
> (84)

Interpretation rests, primarily, on two words: *dumb* (unable to speak and/or unable to think) and *sight* (to see and/or to draw a bead on) and the water imagery that threatens always to overflow Lake Chelan's brim.

The point, of course, is that the relevance of "Lake Chelan" is hardly regional; it can fill up the eyes of a "trapper's child" (generation after generation) with "some irrelevant flood" that, nonetheless, stops him cold. It is as if only the lake's brim can hold water at what Stafford calls the exactness "gravity requires." "Gravity" is yet another pun, a way of playing on human "seriousness" as well as on the laws of physics. And I suspect it is this former meaning, this sense of that "line" (surely a playful nod at Stafford's own *poetic* line) that counterbalances the line-of-sighting from the opening stanzas, that knits the poem into a dramatic unity.

Traveling Through the Dark is filled with poems of movement, simultaneously literal and psychological. In the third section, entitled "Representing Far Places," the title poem raises the old oppositions between wilderness (albeit, one poetically recaptured rather than directly experienced) and society, only to resolve the apparent contradiction in lines 13–14. The effect is sonnetlike, in the structuring of its argument if not in its formal characteristics. Divided into two stanzas, the first six lines efface the canoe's paddler, preferring, instead, to concentrate on those emanations of Nature above and below the water's surface:

> In the canoe wilderness branches wait for winter;
> every leaf concentrates; a drop from the paddle falls.
> Up through water at the dip of a falling leaf
> to the sky's drop of light or the smell of another star
> fish in the lake leap arcs of realization,
> hard fins prying out from the dark below.
>
>   (96)

In this "canoe wilderness" where motions of down-and-up suggest a vertical world, all is joined: the "hard [fish] fins prying out from the dark below," the water dripping from the [Indian?] paddle, the sky's "drop of light," a star's "smell." Here, "far places" are unified, coherent, straight as an arrow.

Such is not the case, however, "in society":

> Often in society when the talk turns witty
> you think of that place, and can't polarize at all:
> it would be a kind of treason. The land fans in your head
> canyon by canyon; steep roads diverge.
> Representing far places you stand in the room,
> all that you know merely a weight in the weather.
>
>   (96)

Generally, Stafford eschews the wordplay that is characteristic of modernist poets, but in this stanza, as the "talk turns witty," puns are as appropriate in the tone as they are integral to his vision. "Far places" are, of course, imaginary constructs, the product of dreams, of the imagination, of poetry. One cannot "polarize" them, either by separating beginnings (the deep waters where fish lurk) from endings (the stars) or by reducing them to a "representational" Polaroid snapshot. This, as Stafford implies, would constitute a "treason," a betrayal, a falsification.

Instead, Nature "fans" through one's brain canyon by canyon, road by road. The landscape, in short, turns interior, represented by stasis ("stand [ing] in the room") and the quiet knowledge that "all that you know [is] merely a weight [wait?] in the weather."

The image suggests quietism, but Stafford hastens to add, in his concluding couplet, that there is no need to fret. Contradictions abound; they are the stuff of modern life. The trick is to realize that "It is all right to be simply the way you have to be, / among contradictory ridges in some crescendo of knowing" (97).

"Interlude" has much the same opposition. In this case, however, an eight-line opening stanza is juxtaposed against a couplet that contains both intimations of "nature imagined" and the "cave of space" we know as the public world. To think of "a river beyond your thought" is, of course, to *imagine,* to go beyond this or that actual river to the essence of river itself.

Even Stafford's imperatives have a gentle, cajoling touch, as if he means to riddle his readers into—and out of—"thought" on this "ritual night" of his poetic making. To be sure, we cannot see this river (its purity "avoiding your sight"), but the lines are ambiguous enough so that it may well be "your thought" that is pure, able to "turn anywhere any rock says":

> Think of a river beyond your thought
> avoiding your sight by being so pure
> that it can turn anywhere any rock says
> but always be ready for the next real call . . .
> (105)

Yet, even that river, once imagined in a purity "so pure / that it can turn anywhere any rock says. . ." is only the beginning:

> and beyond such a river this ritual night
> think of summer weather questioning the corn. . .
> and a face like a news event approaches the world.
> (105)

Indeed, it is this last image that hangs over, that haunts, Stafford's return to the quotidian world—and the regularity—of the poem's concluding couplet:

> Then come back to our cave of space
> and wait for the wonder of that face.
> (105)

This opposition between the "naturalness" of Nature and the arbitrary imprints man puts upon it carries *Traveling Through the Dark* to typical Stafford "conclusions"—those tentative expressions toward

openness, toward expansiveness, toward what Richard Howard calls
"the conventional, the given."[13]

Space, of course, is an inescapable fact of western life, and for the
Stafford who wrote about lonely farmhouses on the Kansas prairies,
loneliness, even existential isolation, simply comes with the human
territory. Nonetheless, in a poem like "At Cove on the Crooked
River" he "represents" far places as surfaces that reflect life at its most
elemental, its most harmonious, its best. Cove is, therefore, "the
kind of place where you might look out / . . . and see trouble walking away"; there, "the river meant something"; there, the trees "act
out whatever has happened to them."

By contrast, civilization is rife with what Eliot called "dissociations
of sensibility" (a phrase, by the way, that Stafford himself neither
would use nor especially approve of). Hence, the speaker would like
to "carve" civilization like this,

> decisively outward the way evening comes
> over the kind of twist in the scenery
>
> When people cramp into their station wagons
> and roll up the windows, and drive away.
>
> (100)

"At Cove on the Crooked River" is yet another example of
Stafford's use of the sonnetlike structure—in this case, one that teases
us into thinking that its concluding couplet will move toward a
Shakespearean resolution. But Stafford's poem is as crooked as the
river; its last line bends backward to lines 9–11 ("the kind of
trees / that act out whatever has happened to them") as well as looks
forward to "that kind of twist in the scenery" when day-trippers make
their way home.

Stafford, I would submit, remains suspended, clinically recording
that exact moment when evening sweeps across both land and people.
To "carve civilization like this" is, of course, precisely what the poem
in effect has done. As the concluding line of "Vocation," significantly
enough the concluding poem in *Traveling Through the Dark,* puts it:
"Your job is to find out what the world is trying to be."

In Stafford's telling phrase, "This dream the world is having about
itself"—this life all of us live, formed by the particulars of its memories and their intimations of the future—includes "a trace on the

plains of the Oregon trail." As the poem unfolds, however, key words like "trace" and "plain" begin to take on larger resonances. *Trace,* for example, suggests not only its primary meaning of "a path or trail through the wilderness," but also "the barely perceivable indication of something"; *plain* is both a flat, extensive landscape and straightforward, frank talk. As the poem's speaker, Stafford stands in an ill-defined, tentative [uncomfortable?] middle, caught between the father who pointed out "a groove in the grass" and the mother who "called us back to the car." The elements of that primal scene—meadowlark, sky, parents, and what Stafford calls "the long line through the plain"—remain. The strong rhyme (*plain/remain*), however muted by its positioning in line 13, causes both the speaker and the reader to stop abruptly. Stafford dangles "helpless[ly]" between father and mother, between the call to exploration and the voice of caution. Significantly enough, though, the father gets the last words in "Vocation" because as Stafford once put it:

Well, the word "vocation" means a calling. It sees writing as an exploration, a discovery of process. I don't see writing as a communication of something already discovered, as "truths" already known. Rather, I see writing as a job of experiment. It's like any discovery job; you don't know what's going to happen until you try it. All life is like that. You don't make life be what you've decided it *ought* to be. You find out what life is *trying* to be.[14]

In this sense "Vocation" is yet another of Stafford's "manifesto" poems, a way of concluding *Traveling Through the Dark* on an open-ended note. Like many another poet, he sees the world as a species of "dream," but in his case that dream is marked by the "traces" and the abiding "remains" of one's past. Particular moments, concrete events, unpremeditated discoveries—these are the stuff out of which poems are made. If Stafford's second collection began "in the middle of things"—as a man encounters a dead deer on the Wilson River Road and suddenly finds himself enmeshed in "dark" complexities—it ends with a "charge" to discover the dream behind the dream, the world that tries to be, and that only those with humility and patience ever see.

Stafford's next book, *The Rescued Year* (1966), plays dark suspicions about a loud and increasingly dangerous age against the quieter landscapes of memory. As the voices we associate with the turbulent mid-sixties grew shriller—those justifying the Vietnam War and those op-

posing it; those who automatically held the over-thirty crowd in con-
tempt and those who hated *any* Whitey, young, middle-aged or
old—it is easy to see why a typical Stafford poem of that time and
place might begin: "You would not want too reserved a speaker."
Nonetheless, as he hastens to explain in "Some Shadows,"
". . . where I come from withdrawal / is easy to forgive." This detached, almost quietistic stance frames the poem, from its self-consciously "tentative" prologue to its biting, even subversive
conclusion:

> Forgive me these shadows I cling to, good people,
> trying to hold quiet in my prologue.
> Hawks cling the barrens wherever I live.
> The world says, "Dog eat dog."
>
> (112)

In the collection's title poem, Stafford "rescues" the Kansas of his
boyhood in the only way a poet can—namely, by writing a poem
about it. There, he insists, "little happened / and much was understood." Poets with a nostalgic itch are always in great supply, but it
is hard to think of others given to celebrating the "dullness" that is
part and parcel of rural Middle-America's life. Stafford does:

> I walked out where a girl I knew would be;
> we crossed the plank over the ditch
> to her house. There was popcorn on the stove,
> and her mother recalled the old days, inviting me back.
> When I walked home in the cold evening,
> snow that blessed the wheat had roved
> along the highways seeking furrows,
> and all the houses had their lights—
> oh, that year did not escape me: I rubbed
> the wonderful old lamp of our dull town.
>
> (117)

But toasty memories of popcorn by the stove and "snow that blessed
the wheat" are not the whole story; Stafford also remembers the
preacher who said "Honor!" with "a sound like empty
silos / repeating the lesson."
    In a similar way, people, even admirable ones, are not likely to
understand the shadows that cling to Stafford's evocations of the

past—to the Uncle Georges and Aunt Mabels, to *The Rescued Year's* first section. Too often such people mistakenly put their trust in technology, as Stafford argues in "Our City is Guarded by Automatic Rockets"; they feel that power alone is sufficient, while he insists that "Power is not enough." But having cited Stafford's bald, unequivocal statement, let me hasten to add that "admirable people" also have a way of turning the blunt into the politically doctrinaire, of too easily seeing Stafford as a comrade-in-arms in the disarmament race. Stafford, I would insist, has a radical, even subversive agenda, but the What and How he thinks worth defending is much closer to the well-springs of art than to the hurly-burly of politics:

> There is a place behind our hill so real
> it makes me turn my head, no matter. There
> in the last thicket lies the cornered cat
> saved by its claws, now ready to spend
> all there is left of the wilderness, embracing
> its blood. And that is the way that I will spit
> life, at the end of any trail where I smell any hunter,
> because I think our story should not end—
> or go on in the dark with nobody listening.
>
> (122)

The last lines remind us, of course, of William Faulkner's Nobel Prize acceptance speech, with its ringing eloquence about "man's inexhaustible voice" and man's capacity to "prevail." Stafford might more modestly put the matter as our continuing need to tell stories, as a later title—*Stories That Could Be True* (1977)—suggests. Given the giddy pronouncements by those in the mid-sixties who envisioned an apocalypse just around the the countercultural corner, *The Rescued Year* occupied a curiously unfashionable place in the poetic pantheon. Stafford, in something of a Roethkean mode, might identify with spawning salmon in "Letter From Oregon" ("The gleaming sides of my train glimmered / up over passes and arrowed through the shoals"), but what was a generation taught to trust nobody over thirty (especially, one's parents) to make of lines like this:

> Justifying space through those miles of Wyoming
> till the wave of the land was quelled by the stars;

then tunnels of shadows led me far
through doubt, and I was home.

(123)

Contemporary life becomes evermore complicated even in the
West, and in poems like "A Documentary from America" and "Out
West," Stafford keeps a sharp, disarming eye out for its incongruities:
the TV cameras that capture the crowd cheering a speech "written by
a committee" or the way Governor Hatfield's arm "was the taffy Oregon pulled." Whatever their respective merits as "occasional poems,"
they strike us now as too dated, too self-conscious, too contrived.
Part of the problem is that Stafford cannot quite resist the fun of
kicking a large, easy target when it's up. On other occasions he will
shoot most of his bolt in the title, as he does in "The Only Card I
Got on My Birthday Was from an Insurance Man."

Indeed, when the corrective itch is upon him, Stafford does far better—and writes much richer poetry—when he effaces himself and lets
a surrogate show, rather than tell. This is essentially what happens in
"At the Klamath Berry Festival," where a sociologist dogs the heels
of an Indian dancer or, even more spectacularly, in the image of a
desert lizard gripping the earth in "At the Bomb Testing Site." There
is a good deal of Stafford in both figures, in their isolation, their
quintessential loneliness, but Stafford himself keeps well on the side-
lines.

The sequence entitled "Following the Markings of Dag Hammarskjold" (then, Secretary-General of the United Nations) was an extended meditation in what Laurence Lieberman calls "the mind of a
magnificent human Other being": ". . . merging his thought with
the mind and spirit of Dag Hammarskjold lifts him [Stafford] entirely out of that insular self and expands his personality as never before."[15]

To be sure, some critics welcomed the apparent departure from
Stafford's familiar stomping grounds with considerably less enthusi-
asm. They urged him to continue in the nostalgic personal mode, but
one could argue just as easily that Stafford, even in musing about
Hammarskjold, abandoned neither the plain voice nor tentative stance
that had become his trademark:

Something has folded into this weather, the gush
a mushroom caused, and all damp land becomes

clung everywhere as the hand tries to let go.
So I try not to learn, disengage because reasons
block the next needed feeling. While others
talk, all of my tentative poems begin
to open their eyes, wistful: they could
grow better! And none carry enough
the burden you lifted, to know for us,
to fear, to act, and just to be.

(133)

Like the Indian at the "Klamath Berry Festival" who persists in his
dance even though Scout troops have been stumbling through their
awkward, inauthentic motions, even though a sociologist is zeroing
in for the academic kill, even though the other festival goers do not
"know" or care, Dag Hammarskjold is emblematic of the walker that
blizzards dignify:

Warm human representatives may vote and
manage man; but last the blizzard will dignify
the walker, the storm hack trees to cyclone
groves, he catch the snow, his brave eye
become command . . .
(from "Walking the Wilderness," 138)

Hammarskjold is such a man and, as such, is akin to Stafford's portraits of Jack London and Ishi, the wild Indian. Such people keep
their deep canyons "unmarked for the world"; they "reach out to God
no trembling hand."

Continuity of this sort lies at the heart of the fablelike poem, "The
Animal That Drank Up Sound." Jonathan Holden suggests that we
substitute "eye" for "animal" and thus develop the correspondence
Stafford sees ". . . between sound and the invisible, his concept of
the imagination as an echo-producing power and his notion of the eye
as the enemy of imagination."[16]

My hunch, however, is that the algebraic substitutions are unnecessary; as Holden points out, Stafford modeled his version of the cre-
ation story on American Indian legends and, not surprisingly, in the
process added a touch of the artist to the proceedings. Thus, the animal that "needed" sound came down and, "instead of making any,"
he drank it up—only to learn painfully, and finally, that silence is

death. If there are echoes in this charming "adaptation," they are, I would insist, of Genesis rather than of criticism.

In Stafford's poem the animal's death leads to a prototype of nuclear winter, as moon replaces sun and "the world / lay still and cold for months." If the poem had come to closure with line 27 ("The sun disregarded the life it used to warm."), Stafford would have added yet another apocalyptic vision to the ash heap. But the "but" of line 28 both introduces the "cricket" and begins a reversal that Holden rightly says "is all those possibilities which the imagination can construe about whatever is invisible." Stafford puts it this way:

> Think how deep the cricket felt, lost there
> in such a silence—the grass, the leaves, the water,
> the stilled animals all depending on such a little
> thing. But softly it tried—"Cricket"—and back like a river
> from that one act flowed the kind of world we know. . . .
>
> (146)

That world, "with its life and sound" returned, balanced precariously between a moon that keeps a cold eye out for the animal and a cricket who waits, listens, and "practices at night."

Given the fact that this poem is followed by "Read to the Last Line" (significantly enough, the concluding poem of *The Rescued Year*), one cannot ignore the bonds that bind poet and reader, poem and prayer, story and human survival. We are all, Stafford insists, "in such a story" or, as he puts it in "Sophocles Says", "History is a story God is telling." All a contemporary poet can do is try "to arrange a kind of prayer for you"—a cricketlike chirp against everything that would drink up sound—and all the reader can do for him, in return, is "Pray for me."

With a few notable exceptions (e.g., "In Sublette's Barn," "Montana Eclogue," "Mornings") the poems in Stafford's next collection, *Allegiances* (1970), have an increasingly familiar look about them: not only in their modest, magazine length (usually twenty to twenty-five lines), but, more important, in the easy way he moves from "occasion" to philosophical pronouncement, from flat particulars to bursts of poetic brilliance. Despite his unassuming manner, he is becoming before our very eyes, as it were, a wise poet. An earlier book like *Traveling Through the Dark* ends with a father's voice imploring him to "find out what the world is trying to be." By contrast, in "Father's

Voice" Stafford remembers a quip from childhood—father had once said, "No need to get home early / the car can see in the dark"—and then elevates it into a principle:

> He wanted me to be rich
> the only way we could,
> easy with what we had.

"Easy" is the operative word, at once a description of his father's "gift" and a shrewd statement about Stafford's own aesthetics.

The difference between "Vocation" and "Father's Voice" is that the former ends with father having the last line, while in the latter, it is Stafford himself who completes the syllogism:

> World, I am your slow guest,
> one of the common things
>   that move in the sun and have
>   close, reliable friends
>   in the earth, in the air, in the rock.
>   (157)

The rub, of course, is that Stafford keeps pressing his claims about such "allegiances" until we begin to wonder if he doth not protest a bit too much. Indeed, a poem like "With Kit, Age 7, at the Beach" gives more room for *poetry* to bring complicated, human matters to a satisfying resolution. To watch the ocean's turbulence is both to feel intimations of Nature's power and reminders of our comparative weakness:

> Standing on such a hill,
> what would you tell your child?
> That was an absolute vista.
> Those waves raced far, and cold.
>   (152)

At seven, Kit needs the assurance that poetry alone can provide. And so when she asks "How far could you swim, Daddy, / in such a storm?" Stafford's answer ripples far beyond the Oregon beach of its setting: "As far as was needed, I said, / and as I talked, I swam" (152).

He discusses the poem's radical shift from the mundane to the metaphorical, the paradoxical, this way:

All the first part of the poem is telling artlessly, directly, simply a succession of encounters in the real world. There's no problem in terms of a reader accepting anything in the early part of that poem: it says we climbed a dune, looked out at the ocean . . . all entirely believable, but the last line— "and as I talked, I swam."—puts the reader in the presence of a statement that cannot be taken on the simple level. So he has to make a reversal and accept it as something metaphorical. There's no particular problem about doing this; you simply *have* to. On the literal level it simply won't work . . . But the whole thing, even from the first . . . *All* particulars reflect something, if looked at alertly enough. The job in writing is the repeated encounter with particulars . . . that reinforce each other—and in that case you have a poem.[17]

True enough—indeed, indisputable—but at least part of the power that the last line packs has to do with the power of language, with the *mouth.* To make the metaphorical claim that "as I talked I swam," is to make language work against its grain; it is, at one and the same time, an insistence that the quotidian can be transcended and a reminder that we are squarely within the world of a "poem."

Many of Stafford's "allegiances" continued to be drawn from his abiding past (e.g., "Monuments for a Friendly Girl at a Tenth Grade Party," "Remembering Althea," "Holcomb, Kansas," "Carols, Back Then: 1935," even the elegiac "At the Grave of My Brother"), but there was also an increasing sense that he was superimposing the moral landscape of small-town Kansas onto the Pacific Northwest. In "A Letter," for example, he uses a form that Richard Hugo would exploit so powerfully in his *31 Letters and 13 Dreams* (1977). He "writes" to Oregon's governor, not to advise or complain, but rather to, in his word, "report" on one of the small towns that have a way of escaping a governor's notice:

> This town has no needs. Not one person stirred
> by the three lights on Main Street. It lay
> so mild and lost that I wanted you to know
> how some part of your trust appears, too far
> or too dim to be afraid.

>   (171)

Stafford's empathies gravitate to such places, as if its "mildness," its very rootedness were a mirror image of his own. And unlike poets, busy governors aren't likely to think of towns like this as agenda items. Hence, the reason for Stafford's "letter":

> You could think of that place annually
> on this date, for reassurance—a place where we
> have done no wrong. For these days to find out
> what to forgive one must listen and watch:
> even our friends draft us like vampires, and it is
> the non-localized hurts that do the damage.
> We have to forgive carefully those demands
> for little helps, those unhappy acquaintance.
> We must manage the ultimate necessary withdrawal
> somehow, sometimes to let the atoms swirl by.
>
> (171)

My hunch is that Stafford's letter-poem was never actually sent to the governor (in such cases, the letter form serves as artifice, rather like the requirements for a sonnet or an ode), but even if it were, I doubt very much if the executive branch would pay much attention to the concluding images of locust tree and frond, river wind and canyon. No doubt Stafford's lines would either end in the crank file or, at best, prompt some underling to draft an officious reply.

Nonetheless, "A Letter" is more than jeu d'esprit. Behind its gentle tones lie the steady insistences of an antagonist, one who champions those "too far / or too dim to demand or be afraid." For Stafford, America's true strength is this endless series of small, independent-living towns, whether they belong to the Kansas of his boyhood or the Pacific Northwest of his adult years.

At the same time, however, he reckons the *costs* of such lives—in effect, standing just to the side of those he presumably admires—and, often, darkly critical notes wrinkle in. For example, Stafford's long history of passive resistance, of conscientious objection, no doubt lies behind his view of the "Pioneer Cemetery" section of "Memorials of a Tour Around Mt. Hood":

> Both sides fought stillness
> but stillness came:
> flintlock, war cry—
> now no name.
>
> Dust holds them; restful

grass grows high:
together they grapple
the real enemy.

Overhead, fighting to break the sky,
planes trace our permanence today:
they can't go fast enough
not to go away.

(175)

Granted Stafford has been interested in the image of jet planes streak-
ing overhead (see, for example, "Watching Jet Planes Dive") from the
beginning, and it is fairly easy to see that "the real enemy" is *always*
Time, *always* mutability, *always* Death, but Mount Hood gives those
large themes a concrete setting.

Stafford is also interested in the "whispers" that tell deeper truths
than loud, public noises. Sometimes (as in "What I Heard Whispered
at the Edge of Liberal, Kansas") his poems "speak memory," to use
Vladimir Nabokov's telling phrase; sometimes the "whispers" come
from Nature itself—unexpected, unable to be prepared for, but cru-
cially important nonetheless. In "Things That Happen," for example,
Stafford contrasts those who feel that when a "great event is coming,"
they should be on their best behavior:

Sometimes before great events a person will try,
disguised, at his best, not to be a clown:
he feels, "A great event is coming, bow down."
And I, always looking for something anyway,
always bow down.

(177)

The strong rhyme that links "clown" with "bow down" is hardly acci-
dental; it betrays one of those common misunderstandings that
Stafford is simultaneously tolerant of (after all, *he* bows down too!)
and shrewdly [subversively?] critical about. Put another way, it is the
difference between the artificial and the exploratory, between the man
who chases after the clichés of highly publicized "great events" and
the one who is content to simply look.

Not surprisingly, genuinely "great events" happen in the life of the
latter:

> We were back of three mountains called
> "Sisters" along the Green Lakes trail
> and had crossed a ridge when that
> one little puff of air touched us,
> hardly felt at all.
>
> That was the greatest event that day;
> it righted all wrong.
> I remember it, the way the dust moved there.
>
> (178)

One need not belabor the fact that *one* of the "Things That Happen" is the making of a poem. For Stafford, the process of writing is so allied to the processes of living that the two are nearly indistinguishable. But "Things That Happen" cuts deeper than the puff of wind that Stafford transmogrifies into verse; it also speaks to his essential isolation—partly a matter of chosen environment (in this case, the trail at Green Lakes), partly a posture he strikes in the face of a shrill, insistent world. Once again I return to the word *radical* as the best term to describe his brand of subversive, poetic behavior:

> No one was ahead of us, no one
> in all that moon-like land.
> Oh, I thought, how hard the world has tried
> with its wind, its miles, its blundering
> stumbling days, again and again, to find my hand.
>
> (178)

Curiously enough, in a poem entitled "Things That Happen," Stafford submerges some events in clouds of ambivalence. Do, for example, his last lines suggest that he extends a hand to the world that would seek his out or, rather, is the suggestion more that he keeps his hand hidden—writing poems perhaps? I would argue that this is a case where tensions are at an equipose, when the impulse toward community, toward fellowship, is set against a soothing, even peaceful isolation.

In this sense, "Things That Happen" is fashioned from the metal (mettle?) Stafford calls "Christianite":

> This new kind of metal will not suffer:

it either holds or bends.
Under stress it acts like a bar, or a hinge.

This metal possesses a lucky way,
always to respond by endurance, or
an eager collapse, and forget.

(178)

How different this substance is from the stiff-necked, the self-righteous. And how characteristic it is of Stafford's poetry, and of Stafford himself. Small wonder, then, that

The impulsive cannot understand it.
Only something romantic or brittle
belongs in their hands.

(179)

"How I Escaped" is yet another version of the dichotomy, one that bears striking affinities to Kafka's "The Hunger Artist." In Stafford's case, however, the circus setting and caged jaguar are dreamlike elements of a more general proposition, namely, "How to be Wild," how to be free. And as his persona gradually *becomes* the jaguar—"swerving, momently aimed"—the poem ends with a line that echoes "With Kit, Age 7, at the Beach." There, Stafford talked as he swam; here, he walks what he means.

His quiet skepticism is perhaps best expressed, though, in the opening lines of "Spectator":

Treat the world as if it really existed.
Feel in the cold what hoods a mountain—
it is not your own cold, but the world's.
Distribute for the multitude this local discovery.

(189)

The "as if" qualifier implies that even the naturalistic world may be so much illusion, but the point is not to catch oneself up in the thick language of metaphysics. Rather, poetry calls us to *act* in the face of uncertain truths and, more important, to act joyfully: "*Treat* the world . . ." Line 2 is, of course, a thinly disguised pun on Mount Hood, that everpresent "fact" of Oregon's Pacific Northwest life. The point, though, is to understand that even *your* cold it not exclusively yours, that even it belongs to the world. This conviction, this aesthetic credo, if you will, is what distances Stafford's work from the best, and worst, of other self-referential poets. And if there is a single line that best describes what many of his poems do—some with brilliance, others more predictably—it is: "Distribute for the multitude this local discovery."

"Local discoveries" are, indeed, what *Allegiances* is about. Stafford's unusual use of the plural suggests wide-ranging commitments, loyalties more various than the general formula of "I owe my *allegiance* (singular) to this-or-that political program, to this-or-that abstract idea."

As he puts it in the introductory poem of *Someday, Maybe* (1973):

> The authentic is a line from one thing
> along to the next; it interests us.
> Strangely, it relates to what works,
> but is not quite the same. It never
> swerves for revenge.
>
> Or profit, or fame: It holds . . .
>
> (201)

Someday, Maybe is a succession of stories, or, more accurately, of dreams that round themselves into life stories:

> Just as in sleep you have to dream
> the exact dream to round out your life,
> so we have to live that dream into stories
> and hold them close at you, close at the
> edge we share, to be right.
>
> (201)

Once again, Stafford remains suspicious of "heroic" stories, imagining instead—in "Hero"—how it would be when an astounded hero returned

> to find his name so honored, schools
> named after him, a flame at his tomb,
> his careless words cherished?
>
> (205)

And it is for much the same set of reasons that he fills his poem "Lecture on the Elegy" with details like "the wilting of a flower / the

passing of the year, the falling of a stone." The dead we elegiacally
mourn merely accompany these particulars. The conceit, in effect,
turns the elegy's conventional sadness around:

> . . . those graceful images that
> seem to decorate the poems, they are
> a rediscovery or those elements
> that first created the obvious feelings. . . .
>
> (206)

"Chosenness"—a word Stafford uses both in its biblical and its
"down-home" senses—derives from acts of volition, from the human
communities human beings created. In a poem like "A Girl Daddy
Used to Know," time recaptured once again makes the boys' hearts
at Liberal High, including Daddy's, go "kerplunck." This girl, with
a shape no hill could duplicate or solve, is the stuff puppy love is
made of—at least in the opening stanza.

What complicates the poem, however, is the larger use Stafford
makes of his father's boyhood infatuation. For example, in the second
stanza he introduces what may be apparent contradictions, or simply
the ambiguities of pronoun reference:

> Her father was no one.
> But once, seeing his hat in the
> Saturday crowd, Daddy thought,
> *He sang her.*
>
> (207)

That *he sang her* implies celebration and, moreover, celebration in a
style radically different from the boys with kerplunking hearts. The
question is *who* sang her: the girl's father (described, initially, as "no
one"), the speaker's father, or, perhaps, the speaker himself, project-
ing his own wishes into this portrait of time poetically recaptured.

Something of Stafford's simultaneous attraction to, and distance
from, homespun values is packed into the ersatz "philosophizing" of
the poem's third stanza:

> The people we choose are
> the chosen people. But you look back,

> you look back, and the stupid heart,
> too dumb, too honest, never gets lost.
>
> (207)

Only a Stafford could bury a tautological line like "The people we choose are / the chosen people" and get away with it. Granted, context makes the essential difference; we assent to Stafford's claim because he has demonstrated—yea, dramatized—its truth in Daddy's "choice" of the girl at Liberal High. And in much the same way that he distrusts "heroic tales," Stafford prefers Daddy's brand of chosenness to the biblical version. Thus, phrase like "the chosen people" is best understood as "the people *we*," rather than God, "choose."

At the same time, however, when we look back—this, in a poem centrally concerned with retrospect, and layered with nostalgia—the terms associated with the choosing heart cancel each other out. On one hand, the heart is "stupid" and "dumb" (presumably speechless as well as ignorant); on the other, it is "honest" and incapable of getting lost. Not surprisingly, the forces of the heart win (Stafford apparently has no difficulty in mustering up enough romantic faith to believe that noble savages can also inhabit the plains of Kansas), but always with a slightly subversive edge, a cool distancing, if you will, running against the grain.

In "A Girl Daddy Used to Know," dazzling, almost metaphysical, images resolve the philosophical conflict:

> When Daddy's family moved away
> the calendar wouldn't turn over.
> For a long time the air he breathed
> wouldn't let go of those hills.
>
> (207)

"Wouldn't" is the key word here, repeated as time presumably stops (yet another function, one supposes, of what the heart can choose) and as space becomes a psychological, rather than a physical, unit of measurement. The effect is a stasis of the sort that sentimental poetry insists upon; it is also an example of what is both risky and representative in Stafford's canon. As he puts it in "Dreams to Have":

> A person mixing colors bends low
> when we walk there. "Why are you

so intent on that bottle you are stirring?"
And then I know: in that little bottle
he has the sky.

(213)

Less self-consciously reflexive than, say, "The Escape" ("Now as we cross this white page together . . ."), less the personal manifesto of, say, "Freedom," the concluding lines from "Dreams to Have" suggest one important direction that Stafford's investigations of dreams-and-art will take. The bottled-up sky of the painter is seen less as potential than as possibility, less as platonic "form" than as idea.

Indeed, dreams lie behind the very notion of *Someday, Maybe,* suggesting a vision in which the paths of vision and the imagination intersect. In this respect, "stories" are vitally important. Without them, human beings become disconnected from history, from the land and, most of all, from themselves. One could, for example, think of Hamlet as a man without a story, as somebody who both investigates, and fights against, the definition of "avenger" foisted upon him by the ghost.

Stories That Could Be True (1977) continues the preoccupation with the fictions we tell and those we need. In the title poem Stafford half-jokingly wonders about those versions of the domestic romance in which the mythopoeic hero is spirited away at birth, reared by people of sturdy, peasant stock, and his royal lineage only "discovered" much later—either by accident, miracle, or a combination of the two. In this case, however, if classical literature provides the conditional situation of the opening lines ("If you were exchanged in the cradle and / your real mother died / without ever telling the story . . ."), Stafford adds the all-important contemporary note:

then no one knows your name,
and somewhere in the world
your father is lost and needs you
but you are far away.

(4)

Disconnected, such a "hero" is reduced to whispering "Maybe I'm a king."

How much better, more humanly satisfying is the condition "At the Un-National Monument Along the Canadian Border." There, the

"battle did not happen"; there, "the unknown soldier did not die,"
And by extension, no hero appeared to foist his "story" on unwilling
people. By contrast,

> This is the field where grass joined hands,
> where no monument stands,
> and the only heroic thing is the sky.
>
> (17)

At such a place, people "celebrate" by "forgetting its name"—and in
that reverence, if you will, Stafford finds all the herohood he requires.

To be sure, the Pacific Northwest has no monopoly on such an attitude. Indeed, in Stafford's case one suspects that it was formed long
ago, as part of his Kansas boyhood. And yet, there is a reverence for
place, for the *land,* that gives a decidedly "Western" feel to Stafford's
work. That note comes through most powerfully in his strong identification with the American Indian. There are, of course, his many
published poems that deal directly with the subject, but I was especially taken by the lines tacked to the bulletin board of his study in
Lake Oswego, Oregon:

> Crowfoot Father
>
> Within the sweep of time, we
> understand each other. In
> the lodge, in the prairie.
>
> Father, it is good being planted
> on this earth. Thank you.
>
> Crowfoot Son.

Indeed, Stafford would probably prefer to be counted as one of our
great American Indian poets than lumped together with David Wagoner and Richard Hugo. As he said in an 3 August 1980 letter,
"Without being jumpy about being tagged regional or NWer type,
I can't myself group Wagoner, Hugo and me as typical of a region
in the way that Tate and others might be Southern etc." True
enough. A poet who eschews "programs" for process, who likes, as
he puts it, to "skate with one foot" through a line, while "riding on
the other" is likely to feel boxed in by too tight a classification. But
in a national literature where points of the compass matter, no one

would think of William Stafford as "eastern" or "southern" or, for that matter, "northern." His poems have been "Report[s] from a Far Place," representing both the Pacific Northwest landscape he inhabits and the psychology he brought there:

> Making these word things to
> step across the world, I
> could call them snowshoes.
>
> They creak, sag, bend, but
> hold, over the great deep cold,
> and they turn up at the toes.
>
> In war or city or camp
> they could save your life;
> you can muse them by the fire.
>
> Be careful, though, they
> burn, or don't burn, in their own
> strange way, when you say them.
>   (209)

RICHARD HUGO
(1972)
Photograph by William Stafford

Chapter Three

Richard Hugo's Triggering Territory

Biographical Sketch

Richard Hugo was born 21 December 1923, in Seattle, Washington. He grew up in White Center (a section of Seattle) and, thus, he is a "native" Pacific Northwest poet in ways that William Stafford and David Wagoner, as transplanted midwesterners, are not. Hugo traces his abiding sense of isolation, of alienation, to childhood feelings that the Pacific Northwest was "near the edge of civilization, almost out of it."[1] Moreover, because he was raised by his grandparents (whose schedules demanded quiet), he early learned the benefits, even something of the joys, of putting words onto paper.

In 1943 Hugo joined the U.S. Army Air Forces and served as a bombardier in the Mediterranean theater. His accounts of these experiences (included in his collection of prose essays, *The Triggering Town*) suggest that he was a reluctant warrior and an inept bombardier, but his Air Medal and Distinguished Flying Cross suggest otherwise.

After the war Hugo returned to Seattle and completed his undergraduate work at the University of Washington in 1948. Three years later he married Barbara Williams and began a long stint as an employee of Boeing Aircraft, one of Seattle's largest industries, that lasted until 1963.

Despite the long hours at Boeing, Hugo's abiding interest in verse writing continued. He took graduate classes with the distinguished poet, Theodore Roethke, and in 1952 completed the requirements for a Master of Arts degree.

His life was divided between a vocation at Boeing and an avocation at his writing desk until 1961, when his first book of poetry, *A Run of Jacks,* appeared. Three years later he was offered a position in the English Department of the University of Montana—Missoula, and Hugo remained both affiliated and identified with that institution until his untimely death in 1982, at the age of sixty-three.

Nineteen sixty-four was also the year that Hugo was included in an influential anthology entitled *Five Poets of the Pacific Northwest*. His second volume of poetry, *Death of the Kapowsin Tavern*, appeared in the following year. He received the first of what would become numerous honors when he was given the Northwest Writers Award in 1966. A Rockefeller Foundation creative writing grant followed for 1967–68.

Good Luck in Cracked Italian (published in 1969) was an immediate, tangible result of Hugo's return, as a civilian, to the Italy he experienced during the war. His next collection of poetry, entitled *The Lady in Kicking Horse Reservoir,* appeared in 1973 and was nominated for a National Book Award in poetry.

In 1974 Hugo married Ripley Schemm, after his first marriage ended in divorce. In the following year he received his second nomination for a National Book Award for a collection of poetry entitled *What Thou Lovest Well, Remains American*. In 1977 he published *31 Letters and 13 Dreams,* and the accumulation and the quality of his work resulted in a prestigious Guggenheim Fellowship for 1977–78.

Hugo's stature as a major American poet was established firmly in 1979, when he not only published his *Selected Poems,* but also a collection of essays on poetry and the teaching of poetry entitled *The Triggering Town*. There was clearly a growing audience for the clear sense and easy manner that made Hugo such an effective director of the University of Montana's creative writing program.

Two collections of his poetry appeared in 1980: *White Center,* a book that points backwards to his Seattle childhood, and *The Right Madness on Skye,* a book set in the Scottish island he lived on during his Guggenheim year abroad.

Death and the Good Life, a mystery novel published in 1981, represented something of a departure in the regular flow of Hugo's poetry; it would be followed by the posthumous publication of another novel, *The Hitler Diaries,* in 1983. In the same year a final volume of poetry, *Sea Lanes Out,* appeared.

Richard Hugo died of leukemia on 22 October 1982, in the Seattle where he was born. He had served as a judge for the Yale Younger Poets Series, had received various fellowships from the American Academy of Poets, and had been one of the founding spirits of *Poetry Northwest,* the distinguished "little magazine" published by the University of Washington. A collection of Hugo's poetry, significantly enough, entitled *Making Certain It Goes On,* was published in 1984.

Themes and Techniques: Richard Hugo's Triggering Territory

". . . I suppose if any region could be said to consistently trigger poems in me it would be the Northwest. In other words, if I were afraid of never writing again, afraid of my landscape failing to provide, I would choose to live in the Northwest thinking failure there would be less likely than in other places."[2]

For a poet like Richard Hugo, landscape and poem are nearly interchangeable terms; the former defines the latter, suggesting or, to use Hugo's term, "triggering" the complicated psychological responses that poetry requires. And for Hugo, the Pacific Northwest was *the* generating landscape, the place closest to the sources of his imagination—whether he was writing about the Seattle of his youth, about the Montana of his adulthood, or even about his extended visits to such far-flung places as Italy or Scotland's isle of Skye. By contrast, David Wagoner and William Stafford "discovered" the Pacific Northwest relatively late in their respective careers—when Wagoner accepted a job at the University of Washington (where his Penn State mentor, Theodore Roethke, was by then firmly established) in 1954 and Stafford moved from San Jose State College to Lewis and Clark College in 1957.

I. B. Singer once remarked that all sensitive people feel uncomfortable in this world, but I would argue that writers experience the disease more keenly. This would be true whether the writer in question happened to grow up on New York City streets, a Kansas farm, or by the shores of Seattle's Lake Washington. But that said, it is always one's particular landscape—its rhythms and special vocabularies, its public values and private whispers—that provides the concrete detail from which art is made. In Hugo's case the Northwest was a great sounding board against which he could conduct a search for identity. As he put it in an interview published less than a year before his death, " . . . I always pick foreign settings that are out of the way. For example, in Italy I lived in the relatively remote South and in Great Britain I chose the western isles of Scotland. Even when I lived in London, in 1968, I usually went out of town for my poems, western Ireland or Cornwall . . . I like feeling just barely a part of civilization when I write."[3]

In a documentary film entitled *In a Dark Time* (McGraw-Hill,

1964), Theodore Roethke talks about the Saginaw, Michigan, of his boyhood in these terms: "The marsh, the mire, was always there—immediate and terrifying. It was a splendid place for schooling the soul. It's *America*." But there was always a sense in which Roethke, the self-declared "happy poet," insisted too much about the healthy, patriotic side of his psyche. Like Hugo, he sought out *edges,* marginal places where American poets seem to be consigned, and where they generally flourish. In Roethke's case lines like "That place among the rocks—is it a cave, / Or winding path? The edge is what I have" (from his poem "In a Dark Time") tell a truth deeper than the once-fashionable term "alienation" can ever say.

No doubt Hugo would have come to "marginality" without any help from Roethke. The conditions of his childhood—understanding early, as only a nine-year-old does, that he was one of the "abandoned" of the world; raised, as he was, by stern, unrelenting grandparents; stumbling, as he did, onto the equation of imagination and freedom that is at once a writer's raison d'être and his strength—provided God's plenty. Later, Roethke added demanding lessons in discipline and form, in technique and control, but one suspects that Hugo would have found these on his own. He had, after all, started early:

My grandfather's job at the Seattle Gas Plant was a menial one and his hours fit the schedule he and grandmother had out of necessity assumed for themselves over a lifetime. And there I'd be, alone, not daring to play the radio for fear it would keep them awake in the small house, nothing to do to amuse myself but to either draw pictures, which I did, or put words on paper, which is, if your definitions are fairly fluid, called writing. My art work showed no promise, so I kept on with the words.

It was a good world in many ways, about as good as a writer could hope for.[4]

In Hugo's case "keeping on with words" meant writing poetry during the hours when he was not officially employed as a "tech writer" for Boeing Aircraft. In an age when young poets, for better or worse, are virtually raised inside the academy, the long stretch of years between his M.A. (1948) and his first teaching position (1964) turned out to be a considerable blessing in thick disguise. If it is true that Boeing Aircraft was developing its now-famous 700 series during those years, it is also true that Seattle still thought of itself as a backwater town, with more affinities to its rough-and-tumble pioneering heritage than to urban sophistication. Hugo found his congenial themes, and something of a "voice," in that northwestern world.

His first collection—*A Run of Jacks* (1961)—divides itself between two obsessions: those ghosts of the heart that haunt, that torment, that can only be exorcized in art; and the cyclical, life-affirming motions of water that make up the rhythms of fishing. As Donna Gerstenberger points out:

The title [*A Run of Jacks*] refers quite clearly to the sea-run trout, the steelhead salmon, for a jack is an immature but sexually precocious salmon who has yet to undergo the extreme physical transformation of the spawning male, whose life-giving act, the discharge of sperm as the female drops her eggs, means imminent death for both of them. The title also surely has in its intention a reference to a run of jacks as a longed-for, winning poker hand. The poet as traveler discovering the substance of his life in the present and in memory has been dealt a hand to play, which clearly is no lucky run of jacks, yet, because of the poet's ability to transform and triumph through art, the book itself becomes a run of jacks.[5]

"I have wedged hard water to validate his skin," the speaker of "Trout" declares, in a poem about how to know a fish. Appropriately enough, it opens the collection, full of demonstrations that Hugo has paid the heavy dues craft demands:

> Quick and yet he moves like silt.
> I envy dreams that see his curving
> silver in the weeds. When stiff as snags
> he blends with certain stones.
> When evening pulls the ceiling tight
> across his back he leaps for bugs.[6]
>
> (3)

"Trout" is a poem of contraries, of paradoxes. In the opening line, for example, words like "quick" and "silt" function as near-rhymes, forcing us to hold radically differing notions of speed in a single image. How, we ask, can this trout be simultaneously "quick" and move as sluggishly as "silt"? What, precisely, *is* the relationship between poet and fish, between speaker and the spoken-about?

No doubt the fish being so meticulously described is a psychological extension of the speaker, in the rough way that, say, Nick Adams's description of the calmly suspended trout tells us much about

his state of mind in Hemingway's "Big Two-Hearted River." But
there are important differences. Whatever alienations Hugo may share
with Hemingway, this is a poem about bonding, about shared conditions. That its images have distinctly sexual connotations—suggesting a world where innocence pays for its maturity with heavy cost,
where spawning and death are inextricably connected—is true
enough, but Hugo's poem, unlike the Hemingway story, is not the
work of a leaver-outer. Hugo "puts in" the trout clinically observed
because those are the terms of his art:

> . . . I have stared at steelhead teeth
> to know him, savage in his sea-run growth,
> to drug his facts, catalog his fins
> with wings and arms, to bleach the black
> back of the first I saw and frame the cries
> that sent him snaking to oblivions of cress.
>
> (3)

The key word, I would submit, is *frame,* as an effort to surround this
canvas of nature with the ordering principles of art. In this sense it
is less the echoes of Hemingway that matter than it is the romantics'
fascination with the bird's wordless song (e.g., Keats's "Ode on a
Nightingale") or the musical possibilities of the wind (e.g., Shelley's
"Ode to the West Wind").

By contrast, poems like "Back of Gino's Place" or "1614 Boren"
are studies in abandoned, desolate places—ruminations in what Hugo
calls "other ways of being":

> . . . Not the poverty
> alone, but other ways of being,
> using basic heat: wood brought in
> by the same sea that is blaring
> wealthy ships to a freshly painted port.
>
> (from "Back of Gino's Place," 18)

Because Hugo's speakers are drawn to scenes of desolation and abandonment, it is easy—perhaps too easy—to fix the sensibility in a single, clinical word: alienation. Let me suggest, however, an alternative, drawn from the opening lines of "Back of Gino's Place":

> Most neglect this road, the concrete torn
> and hunched, purple boxcars
> roasting in the wind or in the sun,
> both direct as brass.
>
> (18)

"Neglect" is not only an apt noun to describe the poem's unfolding scene, but it is also the verb that comes closest to identifying those who avoid such places. "He [the speaker] is right to come here," because only *here* can one see wind or sun "direct as brass," only *here* can one be an "unobtrusive ghost" as mud and wood transmogrify themselves into "the color of the day."

If Hugo tends to write about Nature with the romantic's touch, he is the tough-minded realist when it comes to urban squalor. In "1614 Boren," the address of an abandoned Seattle rooming house, Hugo walks through the debris, asking questions, making careful, uncompromising notes:

> Why could room 5 cook and 7 not?
> These dirty rooms were dirty even then,
> the toilets ancient when installed,
> the light was always weak and flat
> like now, or stark from a bare bulb.
>
> (40)

Hard-boiled detective fiction could not have painted the scene more efficiently, or with a heavier dose of detachment. And yet, an earlier stanza mentions a picture as riddling as it is incongruous: "What does the picture mean, hung there where it is / in the best room. Peace perhaps." Granted, the portrait is hardly high art (in it, a house is half hidden "by poplars, / willows and the corny vines bad sketchers used / around that time"), but it speaks volumes about man's need for art nonetheless.

The result is portraiture within portraiture, the bad sketch of a Netherlands scene framed inside Hugo's rendition of 1614 Boren. But it is also a way of getting to the imagination's powers and its needs, themes that Hugo would continue to speculate about:

> But the picture, where? The Netherlands
> perhaps. There are Netherland canals.
> But are they bleached by sky, or scorched

> pale gray by an invader's guns?
> It can't exist. It's just a sketcher's whim.
> The world has poison and the world has sperm
> and water looks like water, not like milk
> or a cotton highway. There's a chance
> a man who sweated years in a stale room,
> probably one upstairs, left the picture here,
> on purpose, and when he moved believed
> that was the place he was really moving from.
>   (40–41)

To insist that "water looks like water"—rather than, say, like milk or a cotton highway—is to place oneself clearly on the side of the realists. Indeed, the line has the ring of manifesto about it, as if Hugo were making it clear early on that a genuine poetic vision requires nothing less. And yet, to speculate about the picture's owner (from "There's a chance . . ." onward) is to introduce reveries that differ in degree rather than in kind. How are they, essentially, different—the man sweating away his years imagining that man?

In "Neighbor" such identifications take the form of an interior dialogue between the Hugo who describes a drunken neighbor and the Hugo who imagines him—with fondness and with terrible fear—as an extension of himself:

> I admit my envy. I've found him in salal
> and flat on his face in lettuce. . . .
> And I've carried him home so often
> stone to the rain and me, and cheerful.
>   (44)

Salal is a remarkable word worth pondering over. There are any number of "mysteries" in "Neighbor" (the third stanza, for example, is filled with cryptic references to "the good girl—what's her name?"—or the dog this smiling drunk "beat to death that day in Carbonado"), but the risk of "salal" is greater because the word is likely to be unfamiliar to most readers. To choose it is to make a statement about language, about the terms a poet appropriates as part of his native voice. Or as Hugo himself puts it in a revealing piece called "Nuts and Bolts":

Use any noun that is yours, even if it has only local use. "Salal" is the name of a bush that grows wild in the Pacific Northwest. It is often not found in dictionaries, but I've known that word long as I can remember. I had to check with the University of Washington Botany Department on the spelling when I first used it in a poem. It is a word, and it is *my* word. That's arrogant, isn't it? But necessary. Don't be afraid to take emotional possession of words. If you don't love a few words enough to own them, you will have to be very clever to write a good poem.[7]

Wind, rock, stream, and *gray* are other words—admittedly less exotic than "salal"—that find their way, time and again, into Hugo's poems. In a rough way, the same thing is true of his widening network of psychic identifications. If "Neighbor" begins with the image of a polite, smiling drunk who falls in the Hugo garden—one that, no doubt, mythopoeic critics will tell us is a dead ringer for the biblical Garden and the postlapsarian world—it ends with the poet both as secret sharer and chronicler:

> I hear he's dead, and wait now on my porch.
> He must be in his shack. The wagon's
> due to come and take him where they take
> late alcoholics, probably called Farm's End.
> I plan my frown, certain he'll be carried out
> bleeding from the corners of his grin.
>
> (44)

Like the conjunction of water and sperm, renewal and death that dominates the poems about steelhead salmon, there are fusions here: blood and grin, alcohol and death, envy and discreet distance. Notice, too, the words that dominate the final stanza: "I *hear* he's dead" (rather than "know"); "He *must* be in his shack" (rather than "is"); "The wagon's *due* to come" (rather than "will"); "*probably* called" (rather than "called"); and significantly, "I *plan* my frown (rather than, I "frown"). In a typical Hugo poem the speaker rushes in with all the brashness and swagger of a Humphrey Bogart, and exists sounding for all the world like Leslie Howard. What, the speaker wonders, goes on "in that dim warm mind"? And more important, why does he "envy" him? Is it simply because the drunken neighbor is one of the world's outcasts, one of the solid down-and-outers whose disarming honesty appeals to Hugo? Perhaps, but I think there are as many elements of repulsion as attraction, as much that speaks to what its controlled sentimentality covers up as there is to what its elegiac tone reveals.

Hugo, in effect, turns his neighbor into a ghost, which is generally what happens to the people of his early poems. This is especially true of the woman in "The Way a Ghost Behaves" and "The Way a Ghost Dissolves." She is a tough, uncompromising type, the sort who *makes* her garden work

>   because, early on the first warm day
>   while others wait the official end of winter
>   her hoe is ringing rocks away.
>   (from "The Way a Ghost Behaves," 50)

Hugo's readers have long assumed that the figure was modeled on his grandmother, the religiously inclined, strict-minded woman who raised him after Hugo's father walked out and his teen-aged mother could not cope. Not surprisingly, Hugo has denied the autobiographical connection, especially when critics pushed too hard, or too close. That a poet alters, or heightens, the literal facts is, of course, as much a given as his search for interesting words; that Hugo omitted the most revealing of these autobiographical portraits ("Digging is an Art" and "The Other Grave") from his *Collected Poems* points to yet another "truth" poets often protest too much about.

Either way, Hugo's ghost remains:

>   She planted corn and left the rest
>   to elements, convinced that God
>   with giant faucets regulates the rain
>   and saves the crops from frost or foreign wind.
>   (from "The Way a Ghost Dissolves," 54)

Armed against the elements with a combination of old-time religion and hocus-pocus, she fears neither frost nor wart. Moreover, she murders to create her version of the Edenic garden:

>   . . . The earth provided food
>   if worked and watered, planted green
>   with rye and grass every fall. Or driven wild
>   by snakes that kept the carrots clean,

> she butchered snakes and carrots with a hoe.
> Her screams were sea birds in the wind,
> her chopping—nothing like it now.
>
> (54–55)

As Gerstenberger shrewdly points out, ". . . although her garden grows well, descriptions of it do not have the feel of the world of natural growth. Instead, it seems a place where vegetables are commanded to grow and the ground is bent to her and her god's will."[8]

Indeed, what the poem explores are the ways in which ghost and speaker differ. One indicator is the "foreign wind" introduced at the end of the first stanza, only to reappear, transmogrified, in the poem's final lines.:

> And why attempt to see the cloud again—
> the screaming face it was before it cracked
> in wind from Asia and a wanton rain.
>
> (55)

With the exception of a wry remark about warts ("memories or comic on my nose," Hugo interjects, after outlining the stages by which the woman spirited *hers* away), the speaker of "The Way a Ghost Dissolves" keeps himself resolutely effaced, nearly "dissolved" himself. For three stanzas this is a poem in the third person.

The fourth stanza, however, introduces the "I" who will become a prominent feature of Hugo poems. If he had taken shelter behind the persona-with-warts earlier, now is the time "to garden on the double run, / my rhythm obvious in ringing rakes." In short, "The Way a Ghost Dissolves" dissolves into a poem about the making of a poem. As the "ghost" fades, Hugo's poetic consciousness fills the vacuum.

In this sense, then, the final lines are chock-full of double entendres, of language twisted into tricky configurations. *Tone* dominates, in a series of lines that make it impossible to "forget the tone":

> Forget the tone. Call the neighbor's trumpet
> golden as it grates. Exalt the weeds.
> Say the local animals have class
> or help me say that ghost has gone to seed.
>
> (55)

"Tone," of course, refers as much to judgment as it does to sound, as much to what irony whispers as to what the literal words insist upon.

Moreover, in a poem with gardening as its central metaphor, that the
ghost herself has "gone to seed" is *tone* a-plenty.

Finally, there is the business of "dissolving" announced in the
title. As Hugo would have it, the woman has become a cloud, one as
impossible to avoid as any of the nominal statements that preceded
her metamorphosis are literally impossible to believe. God, as it turns
out, did not keep her from the "foreign wind" of line 7; rather, she
persists, as "the screaming face it was before it cracked [like
thunder?] / in wind from Asia and a wanton rain." In this portraiture
Hugo remembers the woman's screams (whether they originally came
from his grandmother or not), but there is also a playful possibility
that his words, artfully arranged, can defuse the terror with a joke.
Hence, his insistence that the Asian wind produces a "wanton" (won-
ton) rain—an odd note, perhaps, on which to end his first book, but
one that would reappear, with more confidence, with more sheer bra-
vado, in later books.

A Run of Jacks was, then, a mixed, but impressive debut. As Richard Howard points out, with equal measures of wit and condescen-
sion, Hugo's first book ". . . proceeds from the very first poem
("Trout") as if the proper study of mankind was fish."[9] But fish are
what Hugo knows, and what Roethkean models taught him could be
turned into serious poetry. If Hugo shared something of the immatu-
rity associated with the jack, he also knew that his particular "run"
was a way of announcing a special vocabulary, a distinctive voice, a
triggering material. And yet, even as he explores the complicated
rhythms of cyclical returns of procreation and death, he tends to seek
out those "edges" that confirm his deep sense of marginality. In
"Duwamish," for example, he finds himself, at last, admitting:

> But cold is a word. There is no word along
> this river I can understand or say.
> Not Greek threats to a fishless moon
> nor Slavic chants. All words are Indian.
> Love is Indian for water, and madness
> means, to Redmen, I am going home.
>
> (46)

At best, *A Run of Jacks* can project a hope that the desolation he has
a nose for is not *all*, that alienation is not the final word in contemporary man's story:

That hermit in the trailer at the field's
forgotten corner, he has moments, too—
a perfect solo on a horn he cannot play,
applauding sea, special gifts of violets
and cream. In bed at 5 P.M.
he hears the rocks of children on his roof
threatening his right to waste his life.

With the Stilli this defeated and the sea
turned slough by close Camano, how can water die
with drama, in a final rich cascade,
a suicide, a victim of terrain, a martyr?
Or need it die? Can't the stale sea tunnel
climb and start the stream again
somewhere in the mountains where the clinks
or trickle on the stones remind the fry
ending is where rain and blackmouth runs begin?
(from "At the Stilli's Mouth," 53–54)

Granted, this is, at best, a wish rather than an affirmation. But in a poet like Hugo such dreams point toward the next books. *A Run of Jacks* made it clear there would be many, many more.

Death of the Kapowsin Tavern (1965) continued Hugo's sojourn through a landscape of impermanence. Like *A Run of Jacks,* these poems tend to find a congenial setting in hideouts and river shacks, amid the burned-out and decayed:

The world goes on with money. A tough cat
dove here from a shingle mill on meat
that glittered as it swam. The mill is gone.
The cat is ground. If I say love
was here, along the river, show me bones
of cod, scales and blood, faces in the clouds
so thick they jam the sky with laughter.
(from "Duwamish Head," 68)

Hugo adopted an elegiac posture early, and it stuck. At a time when the Pacific Northwest was giddy with chance, with the excitement and possibilities generated by its highly successful World's Fair, he set about the task of mournfully praising those buildings and people who resisted. The result, inevitably, was a certain amount of repetition, as if his triggering subjects (the Kapowsin Tavern, for example) were destined to be "studies" in preparation for some future masterpiece.

That reviewers chided Hugo about old river water in new bottles did not especially bother him. As he put it once:

In fact, most poets write the same poem over and over. Wallace Stevens was honest enough not to try to hide it. Frost's statement that he tried to make every poem as different as possible from the last one is a way of saying he knew it couldn't be. (*TT,* 15)

Nonetheless, the very openness of the poems in *Death of the Kapowsin Tavern* suggests that Hugo could narrow the gap between the observer and the observed in ways that were not possible in his first book. By this I mean, the psychological equation established between speaker and landscape turned inward, often in ways that made comic mankind the proper study of man. Consider, for example, "December 24 and George McBride is Dead," a poem that combines elements of elegy with confession, self-mockery with tough-guy sentimentality:

> You a gentleman and I up from the grime—
> now wind has shut your dark, dark eyes
> and I am left to hate this Christmas eve.
> Christ, they're playing carols. Some crap
> never stops. . . .
>
> (87)

A dozen years later Hugo's "letter poems" would refine this plain-talking speech into art of a high calibre indeed, but one can see its embryonic development here. To walk, as it were, on the edge of prose, to write a poetry of bald, uncompromising poetry like "I get along, write my poems. Essentially / a phony" is to risk a good deal, especially in a second book. And while it is true that 1965 produced more than its fair share of "confessional" poems (every poet worth his or her salt had to have a version of Robert Lowell's *Life Studies* [1959] in roughly the same way that painters were once expected to have im-pressionistic renditions of fruit bowls), it was also true that Hugo had joined the University of Montana's English Department only a scant year before. Even a chest-thumping "confessional" poet might have had second thoughts about announcing him- or herself as a "phony" before the tenure vote was in. On that fateful Christmas Eve, Hugo, apparently, could not have cared less.

What makes Hugo's poem work, however, is less its fashionable starkness, its unrelenting candor, than its stances—its alternating tones and rhythms—about the Death Question. Behind the tough-guy swagger ("Christ, they're playing carols. Some crap / never stops"), the catalog of incongruities, lies the loss he mourns as if it were—indeed, in some ways, *is*—his own: "George, it's Christmas eve / and bells are caroling. I'm in the kitchen, / fat and writing, drinking beer and shaking" (87). Hugo adopted a "fat man" persona early, partly from the girth his legendary appetite created (he could polish off a half-gallon carton of ice cream in a single sitting), partly from a need to see the world as an oddity, a comic outsider.

"Eileen" is a more complicated exercise in loss and adjustment, in masks and projective fantasies. Here, it is wind, rather than the carols, that surrounds Eileen's departure. But whether it is the Christmas songs that confound the fact of George McBride's death with the myth of a god's birth or wind "drowning out the car / and raising dust," the end result is much the same, namely, a Hugo left with "shaking hands" and the need for revenge:

> Some day I'll be too big for them to hit,
> too fast to catch, too quick to face the cross
> and go away by fantasy or mule
> and take revenge on matrons for your loss
> and mail you word of faces I have cut.
>
> (85)

One truth, of course, is that the speaker must continue living under oppression's thumb ("I wax their statues, croak out hymns"), but his is a reluctant service, reluctantly given. He will not, for example, show his "hatred to their food"; instead, he waits and shams, plots and dreams:

> . . . knowing
> it was just a bird who crossed the road
> behind you and the sunlight off the car.
>
> (86)

Small wonder, then, that Hugo found himself attracted to spots "the brand new freeway won't go by" or "Road Ends at Tahola." As he puts it in "Duwamish Head," the most ambitious poem of his second book:

> To know is to be alien to rivers.
> This river helped me play an easy role—
> to be alone, to drink, to fail.
>
> (68)

A word like *fail* may not be private in the way that, say, "salal" is, but Hugo uses it in special ways nonetheless. For him, "feelings of worthlessness can give birth to the toughest and most welcome critic within" (*TT*, 70). And in an essay entitled "Statements of Faith," he elaborates on the remark this way:

> Poets who fail (and by fail I mean fail themselves and never write a poem as good as they know they are capable of) are often poets who fail to accept feelings of personal worthlessness. They lack the self-criticism necessary to perfect the poem. They resist the role of a wrong thing in a right world and proclaim themselves the right thing in a wrong world. . . . In a sense they are not honest and lack the impulse (or fight it) to revise and perfect. (*TT*, 70)

Behind the playfulness about failure—those who accept their worthlessness and ironically enough, succeed versus those who fight against feelings of worthlessness and consequently *fail*—lies an elaborate schema for dividing modern American poets into two camps: those with attitudes akin to the Krebs of Ernest Hemingway's "Soldier's Home" and those more akin to the Snopes of William Faulkner's "Barn Burning." As Hugo puts it:

> . . . Krebs, by birth and circumstance is an insider. As a result of his experiences in a war and his own sensitivity, he feels alienated and an outsider. In Faulkner's story, the protagonist, Snopes, a little boy, by birth and circumstance is an outsider who was desperate to be in. (*TT*, 68–69)

The result is a formula that allows Hugo to number William Carlos Williams, Ezra Pound, Wallace Stevens, and Allen Ginsberg in the camp of Krebs while placing T. S. Eliot, Theodore Roethke, Robert Lowell, William Stafford, and James Wright among the Snopeses. To be sure, Hugo's "labels" carry with them all the liabilities that come with the territory of neat, tidy distinctions, but they tell us a good deal about how he views his own work, and that of other Northwest poets. To feel oneself, from the outset, as an outsider is to know the burden of potential betrayal, or, as Hugo puts it: "The Snopes poets would feel that their heritage has some deep emotional claim to their loyalties. The Krebs poets could write their best poems without fingering their fathers" (*TT,* 69).

This complicated rhythm of loss and recovery, perhaps more than anything else, explains the psychic energy that lies behind the opening stanza of "Death of the Kapowsin Tavern":

> I can't ridge it back again from char.
> Not one board left. Only ash a cat explores . . .
>
> . . . The white school up for sale
> for years, most homes abandoned to the rocks
> of passing boys—the fire, helped by wind
> that blew the neon out six years before,
> simply ended lots of ending.
>
> (102)

Hugo is drawn to such landscapes, places where a final conflagration "simply ended lots of ending," as if poetry alone could somehow "ridge it [the tavern, the town, the Northwest itself?] back again from the char."

As he puts it, in the vernacular of the tough-guy: "A damn shame." Now there is nowhere for the chilled troller to go for "bad wine / washed down frantically with beer"; now there are no wise men left to tell about the cranes on their "two-mile glide" or to name the "nameless yellow / flowers thriving in the useless logs."

And yet, the Kapowsin Tavern has its elegiac spokesman, its *poem,* if you will—partly out of Hugo's affection for what the Northwest was and his loyalty to what it stood for; partly out of his deep-rooted belief that "Nothing dies as slowly as a scene" (102). To record its death pangs is to place oneself on an edge, to be in equipoise with past and present. It is also to "fail" (that word again!), and, furthermore, to build in one's failure as an essential component of the poem's fabric:

> The dusty jukebox cracking through
> the crackle of a beered-up crone—
> wagered wine—sudden need to dance—
> these remain in the black debris.

> Although I know in time the lake will send
> wind black enough to blow it all away.
>   (102)

Here are "winds in the wind" [Roethke's title] with a vengeance. Indeed, *wind* frames the poem, from the windswept fire of the first stanza to those winds that will sweep away even the tavern's black debris in its concluding one. Nonetheless, Hugo's poem is a hedge against the certain future, a way of digging one's heels in familiar soil. Of such passions are poems of the Northwest made. Hugo's second book was thoroughly "regional" in that worthy sense.

By contrast, Hugo's next collection, *Good Luck in Cracked Italian* (1969), explored landscapes at a far remove from the world of rivers and steelhead, abandoned buildings and desolate northwestern places. Strictly considered, then, one can only agree with Gerstenberger's assessment that the book "has little relevance to his identity as a Western writer."[10] At the same time, however, what Ralph Waldo Emerson said about travel ("My giant goes with me wherever I go.") is equally true for Richard Hugo. *Good Luck in Cracked Italian* is an exercise in postures transplanted, in attitudes tested out against landscapes that are simultaneously "foreign" and all too familiar. As Hugo puts it:

The 1944 Italy I remembered [from his World War II days as "the world's worst" bombardier] brown and gray and lifeless. Every city, every small town reeked. No young men in the towns and no cattle in the fields. The war had taken the men and the Germans had taken the cattle. That was the Italy I expected to find when I came back. I hate to admit it, but that was the Italy I wanted to find. I fell in love with a sad land, and I wanted it sad one more time.

I must confess to a perverse side of self. I give and give to beggars, but there is in me something that feeds on the now of things. Of course I want it all better, want poverty gone forever from the world. But I also have the urge to say, "Stay destitute three more days, just until I finish my poem." I'm ashamed of that in me. (*TT,* 76)

The "cracked" Italian of his title refers both to Hugo's difficulties with the language (the *gn* sound, he tells us, was especially troubling), and to certain moments, certain images, he would later share with his psychiatrist and explore in poems like "Centuries Near Spinnazola" (from *A Run of Jacks*) or "Index" (from *Death of the Kapowsin*

Tavern). In short, there were "Italian" poems before there was a collections called *Good Luck in Cracked Italian,* but it is also fair to say
that the earlier poems were preliminary sketches, ways of warming up
for more substantial performances.

One of the first surprises that the writing of *Good Luck in Cracked
Italian* brought was Hugo's realization that the sad landscape he remembered, and identified with, had virtually disappeared, and without so much as a by-your-leave from Hugo:

> Now it's clean. The whores seem healthy.
> and the bombed-out panes have been replaced.
> This arcade's a monument to money,
> in a city with a desperate need
> for money, in a country with no need at all
> for love. These shops will never sell
> those gaudy chandeliers. The gaudy whores
> display themselves forever with no takers.
> (from "Galleria Umberto I," 129)

Hugo remembers the Galleria as "a little more forlorn," as an Italian
equivalent of those run-down locales he had searched out, and found,
in the Pacific Northwest. If Hugo could not see himself as a poet of
boosterism—celebrating, say, Seattle's Space Needle or the glitzy
night spots that had cropped up along Skid Row—neither could he
imagine himself finding poetic material in the tourist traps a once-
ruined land can build twenty years later.

Memory, however, speaks simultaneously of what was and of what
continues to be, the deeper human condition:

> It was here that John Horne Burns
> saw war summed up, the cracked life
> going on, taking what it would in gesture
> and a beggar's bitter hand.
>
> (129)

In the earlier "Italian" poems Hugo had prided himself both on his
posture as the tough guy and on his ability to write tough, intellectually demanding poems. As he puts it in "Ci Vediamo," a revealing
essay about the two Italies he experienced, and how he turned them
into art,

. . . Note how definite the voice is [talking about "Index"]. How strong the
command to the self tries to be. How the poem urges the man in it to accept
reality in all its cruelty and diffuseness. And I even took a private pride in
the difficulty of the poem. I wasn't afraid of anything. No, sir. You don't
understand my poems? Screw off, Jack. But in real life, be my friend. Like
me. Like me. (*TT*, 80–81)

To compare a stanza from "Index" with one from a later poem like
"Spinazzola: *Quella Cantina La*" is to understand the difference between an ambitious, albeit clotted, poetic texture and the simplicity,
the sheer clarity of voice, that would dominate Hugo's mature work:

> The sun is caked on vertical tan stone
> where eagles blink and sweat above
> the night begun already in the town.
> The river's startling forks, the gong
> that drives the evening through the pass
> remind the saint who rings the local chime
> he will be olive sometime like a slave.
> (from "Index," 73)
>
> . . .
> A field of wind gave license for defeat.
> I can't explain. The grass bent. The wind
> seemed full of men but without hate or fame.
> I was farther than that farm where the road
> slants off to nowhere, and the field I'm sure
> is in this wine or that man's voice. The man
> and this canteen were also here
> twenty years ago and just as old.
> (from "Spinazzola: *Quella Cantina La*," (124)

The rub, unfortunately, is that Hugo is *too* good a storyteller, especially when his prose pieces fill in the background and circumstances
on which the Italian sequence is propped. There are even times when,
shameful to say, we prefer the Hugo who writes about Hugo to the
Hugo who writes his poetry.

But that said, let me hasten to add that there are important poems
in Hugo's third book, poems that he not only *had* to write (as if his
war years would, somehow, have been incomplete, and inconclusive,
without them), but also poems that showed a greater willingness to
take genuine risks, to reveal the psyche more deeply, more discursively than earlier poems do:

> There's no metaphor for pain, despair.
> It's just there. You live with it, if lucky
> in a poem, or try to see it, how it was
> under this dome roof with children dead,
> the stench of death blown at you
> off a sea we should have asked for wisdom
> by wind we still should beg for tears.
> In all our years, we come to only this:
> capacity to harm, to starve, to claim
> I'm not myself. I didn't do these things.
>   (from "Galleria Umberto I," 129)

Hugo's next book, *The Lady in Kicking Horse Reservoir* (1973), turned his attention to the Montana he had called home since he joined the University of Montana's English Department in 1964. In an essay entitled "The Writer's Sense of Place," he talks about the vexing problem of "regionalism" this way: "I am a regionalist . . . though of course there are several ways of defining region. When I write a poem, I lay emotional claim to the setting." *The Lady in the Kicking Horse Reservoir* is filled with efforts at surveying the landscape and staking out one's poetic "claim." The record, oddly enough, begins in Italy, where Hugo "imagines" a map of Montana's "state"— this while his efforts to understand the war by juxtaposing the Italy of 1964 against the one he suffered through twenty years earlier continue:

> The two most interesting towns, Helena, Butte,
> have the good sense to fail. There's too much
> schoolboy in bars—I'm tougher than you—
> and too much talk about money. . . .
> [By contrast, here in Italy] no one fights
> in bars filled with pastry. There's no
> prison for miles. But last night the Italians
> cheered the violence in one of our westerns.
>   (165–66)

In effect, "A Map of Montana in Italy" bridges Hugo's third and fourth books, at once an overview and a retrospective, a way of dovetailing the violence he remembers from the war with the romance of violence indigenous to the West.

On the simpler levels of popular culture, one could, I suppose, explore the phenomenon of "spaghetti Westerns" [low-budget Italian versions of the Hollywood shoot-'em-up, filled with cowpokes and gunfighters] that were flourishing when Hugo was writing his poem, but that would be to miss the richer sides of Hugo's vision.

To understand the Montana landscape is to understand the relationship between isolation and meanness, between space and the cruelty that too often fills it up:

> With so few Negroes and Jews we've been reduced
> to hating each other, dumping our crud
> in our rivers, mistreating the Indians.
>
> (165)

Even more important, Montana is big enough, *harsh* enough, to square with Hugo's aesthetic of abandoned placed and large, desolate stretches. It became, if you will, his triggering state. As Gerstenberger points out:

The [Montana] landscape is wider than it was in the state of Washington, the spaces between bars and towns greater; all in all, a more comfortable correlative for loneliness than the richly lush, overgrown, and forested Puget Sound region.[11]

Something of this "comfortable correlative for loneliness' can be seen in the general atmosphere of "Silver Star," a poem that insists abandonment applies equally to machines and to men:

> This is the final resting place of engines,
> farm equipment and that rare, never more
> than occasional man. Population:
> 17. Altitude: unknown. . . .
> Old steam trains
> have been rusting here so long, you feel
> the urge to oil them, to lay new track, to start
> the west again.
>
> (177)

Hugo, in short, continues to find measures of congenialty in these forlorn spots. As he says in "The Milltown Union Bar" with its revealing epigraph: *(Laundromat & Cafe)*

> You could love here . . .
>
> You need never leave. Money or a story
> brings you booze.
>
> (166)

The poem's final line is even more revealing, given the tentative, unsteady nature of Hugo's childhood: ". . . Doors of orphanages / finally swing out and here you open in."

But if Hugo kept his fingers pressed, again and again, on by now familiar themes, if the run-down, the desolate, had become a trademark, he wrote with greater verbal subtlety, with finer discriminations of *ear*. Consider, for example, the opening stanza of "Indian Graves at Jocko," paying particular attention to the ways that sound and sense are inextricably combined:

> These dirt mounds make the dead seem fat.
> Crude walls of rock that hold the dirt
> when rain rides wild, were placed with skill
> or luck. No crucifix can make
> the drab boards of this chapel Catholic.
> A mass across these stones becomes
> whatever wail the wind decides is right.
>
> (179)

Because the poem's ostensible subject—Indian graves— is the stuff of which symbol and metaphor can be too easily fashioned, Hugo takes a tougher, more honest tack. His use of slant rhymes, for example (fat/dirt, luck/crucifix/Catholic), keep the sentimental, the melodramatic, at arm's length. Moreover, a word like "mass" tells us worlds about the essential difference separating Indian from white man, the cycle of nature from Catholic ritual. The *true* mass, Hugo implies, is wind over rock (also, of course, an indicator of "mass," of solidity and weight), wordless "words" that speak more eloquently than anything said in the clapboard chapel:

> They asked for, got the Black Robe
> and the promised masses, well meant
> promises, shabby third hand crosses.

> This graveyard can expand, can crawl
> in all directions to the mountains,
> climb the mountains to the salmon
> and a sun that toned the arrows
> when animals were serious as meat.
>
> (179)

As Hugo puts it in "Montgomery Hollow": "You conquer loss / by going to the place it happened / and replaying it." That, it seems to me, is as good a description as any of what the quintessential Hugo poem does:

> To know a road you own it, every bend
> and pebble and the weeds along it,
> dust that itches when the August hayrake
> rambles home. You own the home.
>
> (191)

Small wonder, then, that Hugo, being Hugo, turns the Montana Indians into what Gerstenberger calls "central symbols for the dispossessed and despairing."[12] They are, in effect, grotesque extensions of himself. At the same time, however, to "own" their experience imaginatively is to realize how complicated, how slippery, a term like "defeated" is. Was Chief Joseph wrong to choose a defeated life over the certainty of death? Or, perhaps more to the point, in his own fashion is Hugo?

Such questions are central to the arc of emotions in the collection's title poem, "The Lady in Kicking Horse Reservoir." To be sure, its Indian name is an appropriate northwestern detail, but it also suggests a link to larger rhythms of defeat and reconciliation. On one level, of course, this is a "portrait of a lady" who has deserted him, a bitter testimony to a love affair gone sour. In this sense, "The Lady in Kicking Horse Reservoir" ranks among the most personal of Hugo's poems, especially if one sees him as an avatar of the "kicking horse." It is also, more simply, a revenge poem—a poetic species that makes teachers of literature uncomfortable. Witness that delicious anecdote from Hugo's "In Defense of Creative Writing Classes":

A young recent Ph.D. asked me to attend his class to discuss some of my poems with his students. I liked the young man and was pleased he wanted to teach my work. It was a good class. The teacher had done his work well.

That was obvious from the enthusiastic attention the students brought to the work being discussed and the intelligent way they made points.

One student asked how I'd come to write "The Lady in Kicking Horse Reservoir," one of the poems they were studying. My answer was straightforward. I'd had a love affair. The woman dumped me for someone else. I was brokenhearted and vengeful, but cowardly. So in real life I suffered but in the poem I had my revenge—at least early in the poem.

A few days after the class, the teacher told me he had been very surprised at my answer, that he didn't know poets used life that way. I was surprised at his surprise and asked him where he'd assumed poems came from. He replied that he'd believed that a writer sits alone in a room and makes things up. (*TT*, 60)

The well-meaning instructor took his clues from, say, Cleanth Brooks and Robert Penn Warren's *Understanding Poetry,* a textbook that insisted poems lived in an antiseptic realm where the messy facts of biography, of life, would never dare to intrude; Hugo, on the other hand, sounds like a page from Freud's thesis about sublimation and the creative impulse. No doubt Hugo's biographer will give us the lady-in-question's name when he gives us the 400-plus pages of relentless detail we have come to expect in contemporary biography, but will it significantly change our reading of the poem's angry opening stanza?:

> Not my hands but green across you now.
> Green tons hold you down, and ten bass curve
> teasing in your hair. Summer slime
> will pile deep on your breast. Four months of ice
> will keep you firm. I hope each spring
> to find you tangled in those pads
> pulled not quite loose by the spillway pour,
> stars in dead reflection off your teeth.
>
> (201)

For some people, even death is not good enough, not sufficient retribution for the pain they've caused. Apparently, the fickle lady in Hugo's craw is such a beast. The *"now"* that governs the opening lines—with the small brush strokes of meticulous detail (e.g., ten bass)—simply won't do. Rather, Hugo must go beyond these conditions to imagine (project?) her stuck forever in a static, ever-so-slowly decaying future tense: "Summer slime / *will* pile deep on your breast. Four months of ice / *will* keep you firm," etc.

But revenge, however much it might set a poem in motion, cannot reach beyond the wounded self, cannot engage deeper seriousness. In this sense, revenge is not only "cowardly" (to use Hugo's phrase) because it enacts "victories" in art rather than life, but also because revenge delimits the poem per se. The problem, then, is to transcend the weight of conditions—those of the landscape as well as those of the psyche:

> Landlocked in Montana here
> the end is limited by light, the final note
> will trail off at the farthest point we see,
> already faded, lover, where you bloat.
> (201)

Past and present line up, side by side, in the fourth stanza, at exactly the poem's halfway point. There the speaker seems stuck (like the lady in the reservoir?) between memory and desire, between what should be and what *is,* between a conditional future and an insistence about the past:

> All girls should be nicer. Arrows rain
> above us in the Indian wind. My future
> should be full of windy gems, my past
> will stop this roaring in my dreams.
> Sorry. Sorry. Sorry. But the arrows sing:
> no way to float her up. The dead sink
> from dead weight. The mission range
> turns this water black late afternoons.
> (201–2)

The water image links Kicking Horse Reservoir (and its world of adult disappointment) with a memory from childhood when

> One boy slapped the other. Hard.
> The slapped boy talked until his dignity
> dissolved, screamed a single 'stop'
> and went down sobbing in the company pond.
> I swam for him all night. My only suit
> got wet and factory hands went home.
> No one cared the coward disappeared.
> Morning then: cold music I had never heard.
> (202)

If revenge is the easy wish of this poem, to accept defeat is its harder truth, for surely Hugo is the slapped boy "he swam for . . . all night." No doubt his indefatigable biographer will one day tell us who the boy who slapped hard was, but, like the lady's name, it does not really matter. The point is that Hugo breaks through the tough-guy posture that launches the poem, that he can imagine a "vague" hope, that the lady's bones *may* be "nourished by the snow"—in short, that Nature might exercise a healing, transcendent function.

As Hugo liked to put it: "Humphrey Bogart going in and Leslie Howard coming out." If "The Lady in Kicking Horse Reservoir" begins in stasis, in the paralysis of hatred, it ends with images of movement and intimations of resurrection. The lady, for example, spills out "into weather," a

> lover down the bright canal
> and mother, irrigating crops
> dead Indians forgot to plant.
> (202)

She becomes, in effect, part of the cycle, rather than a grotesque plaything of winter's ability to freeze and summer's capacity to entangle her within in "pads." And as for the speaker? He imagines himself sailing west, to a spot where naked Dollys tease oil from whales with their tongues. An image as powerful—and as sexual—as this suggests a speaker who is no longer either frightened or embittered. Even more important, despite the confessional pain of the opening stanzas, there are indicators aplenty that Hugo knew the difficult directions where health lies.

Finally, there is "Degrees of Gray in Philipsburg," probably the most widely anthologized, and best known, of Hugo's poems. It is simultaneously a culmination of earlier efforts (e.g., "Death of the Kapowsin Tavern") at poking among the ashes of desolate places, an impressive demonstration piece for his homegrown aesthetic about "triggering towns," and, interestingly enough, a departure from what threatened to become a rehearsed response, an easy formula for grinding out successive poems.

In the title essay of Hugo's prose collection, *The Triggering Town,* he puts it this way:

The poem is always in your hometown, but you have a better chance of finding it in another. The reason for that, I believe, is that the stable set of knowns that the poem needs to anchor on is less stable at home than in the town you've just seen for the first time. At home, not only do you know that the movie house wasn't always there, or that the grocer is a newcomer who took over after the former grocer committed suicide, you have complicated emotional responses that defy sorting out. With the strange town, you can assume all knowns are stable, and you owe the details nothing emotionally. However, not just any town will do. Though you've never seen it before, it must be a town you've lived in all your life. You must take emotional possession of the town and so the town must be one that, for personal reasons I can't understand, you feel is your town. (*TT*, 12)

Philipsburg was precisely that sort of place. But more to the point, Hugo found it—or more likely, if found *him*—when "he" (by that I mean, his *voice*) was ready. As he explained in an interview:

. . . The Philipsburg poem was actually the culmination of a kind of writing. It was the poem I had been trying to write for twenty years. Of course, these things aren't neat and you don't realize that at the time you write the poem. You try to keep writing that way, but eventually that was the best of all those poems, "West Marginal Way," "Duwamish." Everything just fell into place one day, all within four hours, from five in the morning until nine. I had been in Philipsburg only three hours the day before, and that was the only time I'd been there.[13]

For Hugo, a place like Philipsburg goes through him, rather than the other way around. Indeed, it is the sort of town you search out—that is, if the "you" is Hugo—when your "life broke down," when "the last good kiss / you had was years ago," when the tug that draws you there goes beyond metaphor. Everything about it, everywhere your eye and heart cast themselves, is *you*:

> . . . You walk these streets
> laid out by the insane, past hotels
> that didn't last, bars that did, the tortured try
> of local drivers to accelerate their lives.
> Only churches are kept up. The jail
> turned 70 this year. The only prisoner
> is always in, not knowing what he's done.
>   (216)

To this by now familiar Hugo landscape, "Degrees of Gray in Philipsburg" brings new, even surprising, realizations. For example,

when the third stanza opens with "Isn't this your life?" our expectation is that the series of questions that follow are entirely rhetorical:

> . . . Isn't this defeat
> so accurate, the church bell simply seems
> a pure announcement: ring and no one comes?
> . . . Are magnesium
> and scorn sufficient to support a town,
> not just Philipsburg, but towns
> of towering blondes, good jazz and booze
> the world will never let you have
> until the town you came from dies inside?
>
> (216–17)

Yes, we find ourselves thinking, *this is my life, my Philipsburg! How
did Hugo know it—and me—so well?*

But there are, in fact, *degrees* of gray, not all of them identical. Appropriate the run-down-ness of Philipsburg as one will, it is *still* not
Hugo, not *you*. Honesty (always at the center of whatever aesthetic
Hugo happened to be championing at the moment) demands that this
poem "Say no to yourself." And with the plain, bare line that begins
the concluding stanza, Hugo raises "Degrees of Gray in Philipsburg"
to a seriousness that had escaped even the most artfully done of his
previous studies in "triggering towns":

> The car that brought you here still runs.
> The money you buy lunch with,
> no matter where it's minted, is silver
> and the girl who serves your food
> is slender and her red hair lights the wall.
>
> (217)

We are reminded of, say, the George Orwell intellectually slumming
his way through *Down and Out in Paris and London,* rather than of the
Sylvia Plath who could never quite discriminate between adolescent
suffering and concentration camp victims. Put another way, Hugo's
twenty-year effort to write "Degrees of Gray in Philipsburg" was a
victory that a happy combination of "voice," poetic control, and maturity wrought. It boded well for the collections that followed during
the nine short years that remained.

What Thou Lovest Well Remains American (1975) is a sustained effort
to give the devils of Hugo's past something of their due. One's childhood memories, rather like one's first psychological impressions of a
decaying Philipsburg, are not always, or even likely to be, the *whole*
story. In "A Snapshot of the Auxiliary," for example, an old photo
album initially confirms a world filled with ogres, and the old:

> . . . It is easy
> to see they are German, short, squat,
> with big noses, the sadness of the Dakotas
> in their sullen mouths . . .
> None of them seem young. Perhaps
> the way the picture was taken. Thinking back
> I never recall a young face, a pretty one.
> My eyes were like this photo. Old.
>
> (221)

But if this is *one* photograph, the "next one in the album / is our an-
nual picnic. We are all having fun." Which, then, does the poem's
title refer to? Which is truer, more honest to the experience of
Hugo's childhood? On which photograph does the sly shadow of irony
fall?

Our temptation, of course, is to imagine that Hugo is being playful when he ponders what the picnic means, and meant—and that he
is in dead earnest earlier. But *What Thou Lovest Well Remains American*
is confession with a difference, a wry twist, as it were, on the poems
that have gone before. As he puts it in "Saying Goodbye to Mrs.
Noraine":

> It turned out I remembered most things wrong.
> Miss Holy Roller never had
> an illegitimate son. The military father
> had been good to animals and the Gunthers
> were indifferent to Hitler when we stoned
> their house. . . .
>
> (222)

For Hugo, the places and people of his childhood continue to function
as ghosts of the heart, as abiding presences. But, now, bitter certainty gives way to ambivalence and, in complicated ways, to love.

In their impoverished, even desperate world, is a strength that Hugo finds attractive, even *American*. As the title poem puts it:

> . . . Poverty was real, wallet and spirit,
> and each day slow as church. You remember threadbare
> church groups on the corner, howling their faith
> at stars, and the violent Holy Rollers
> renting that barn for their annual violent sing
> and the barn burned down when you came back from war. . . .
>
> (235)

By contrast, the new, the improved, the good-looking, and the well-fed remind Hugo of the train his wife "took one day forever, some far empty town, / the odd name you never recall. The time 6:23. The day: October 9." This world is no longer his. Indeed, what remains is, ironically enough, the fellowship formed and tested by a very different American Dream, one in which you suddenly discover that

> You loved them well and they remain, still with nothing
> to do, no money and no will. Loved them, and the gray
> that was their disease you carry for extra food
> in case you're stranded in some odd empty town
> and need hungry lovers for friends, and need feel
> you are welcome in the secret club they have formed.
>
> (236)

In *What Thou Lovest Well Remains American* biblical rhythms ("thou," "lovest") reenforce the fundamentalist world that formed him. And in a similar way, the use of the second person pronoun marks a mid-stage between his earlier dependence on the third-person and the first-person pronoun that would become the identifying feature of his final poems. Hugo insisted that the choice had to do with *stance* and, of course, with the sort of poem he was after, but it was a matter he was never entirely comfortable talking about or that he felt he could answer adequately:

I know I would fall into one person or another at any one time. For a long time I was using "you" poem after poem. [See, for example, *What Thou Lovest Well Remains American*.] The psychology of the person enables you to talk; when you say "you," you're able to say certain things that you aren't able to say when you use "I," and vice versa. Now I'm back to using "I" a little more.[14]

Hugo—especially in his later years—became a decidedly public poet, unafraid of speaking out with candor about the messier, less attractive aspects of his life. Again, honesty was the keystone of his aesthetic. *"How you feel about yourself,"* he once wrote, "is probably the most important feeling you have." To "let go"—of bitterness, of hatred, of blame—is as important, perhaps *more* important, as cataloging the indignities of childhood. To love all, despite all, may be one of the benchmarks that separates the great poet from his more limited counterparts. Granted, Hugo, for all the tugs toward sentimentality in his poetry, did not give himself over to "love" easily; he was no bleeding heart, whether the subject at hand was victimized Indians or solid down-and-outers, the Pacific Northwest or himself. Moreover, he knew full well that there was a difference between the demands of autobiography and those of a lyric poem. *What Thou Lovest Well Remains American* tests out strategies for confronting the past that was and the self that is. To read the volume as pure biography (if such an animal exists) would be a mistake; to read it as pure lyric would be to err in the other direction. As Hugo once put it, "In a poem you'll fictionalize something just to see where the possibilities of language take you." In this case the "possibilities" took him outward, to what is perhaps his most "American" of his collections.

The volume *31 Letters and 13 Dreams* (1977) followed Hugo's nervous breakdown while he was a visiting professor at the University of Iowa (in "Goodbye, Iowa," a poem included in *What Thou Lovest Well Remains American,* he writes: "Miles you hated her. Then you remembered what / the doctor said: really a hatred of self.")—at once a "reaching out" to old friends (mostly fellow poets), an assessment of his work thus far, and, most important of all, a sustained attempt to break free from the isolation that, in fact, had imprisoned him.

Hugo's "letter poems" were enormously popular when the first ones appeared in *American Poetry Review.* They seemed so off handedly casual, so effortless, so entirely convincing in voice, in tone, that a wide variety of poets began to imitate them. And small wonder: correspondence has an honored place in the history of the novel (one thinks of everything from epistolary efforts like *Pamela* to contemporary variations like *Herzog*), but the formal demands of poetry erected barriers at every turn. This, despite the clear inclination of contemporary poets to talk directly, discursively, even "formlessly."

Hugo's letter poems were a way of getting to the heart of the psychological matter in ways that the confessional poets of the 1960s could only dream about:

> Dear Condor: Much thanks for that telephonic support
> from North Carolina when I suddenly went ape
> in the Iowa tulips. Lord, but I'm ashamed.
> I was afraid, it seemed, according to the doctor
> of impending success, winning some poetry prizes
> or getting a wet kiss. The more popular I got,
> the softer the soft cry in my head: Don't believe them.
> You were never good. Then I broke and proved it.
> (from "Letter to Kizer from Seattle," 275)

Art is, above all else, an illusion and Hugo's letter poems made it "look easy." What could be easier, after all, than dashing off a letter to a good friend and then breaking the lines until they had the look, the *feel,* of a poem?

Curiously enough, Hugo began to have doubts of his own, especially when the letter poems clustered into a definable grouping. As he put it:

I made a mistake in that book [*31 Letters and 13 Dreams*]. When the first letter poems were published in *American Poetry Review,* they were enormously popular. I got some fan mail and I forced some poems to fill out the book. I didn't realize I was doing that at the time, but I think I wrote several letter poems when I had no impulse to write. This is unforgiveable for someone who has written as long as I have. [15]

Indeed, Hugo much preferred the dream poems and, no doubt, would have been happier had the book been titled *13 Letters and 31 Dreams.* But this is a case, I would submit, where even a thoughtful poet can misjudge his best work. That the letter poems came too easily, that he found himself writing them "to order" and by formula may be true enough, but what counts, in the final analysis, are the results. And the letter poems, as a grouping, tell us much about Hugo and the way he converted experience into art. As readers of contemporary poetry, we would be poorer without them.

Here, for example, is Hugo explaining, once again, the desolate feeling that overcomes him as the landscape of certain western towns crowds in:

> . . . It looks like several towns
> in Montana. Columbus, for one. Even, a little, like the edge
> of Billings. You know. On one side, stores, cafes, a movie
> theatre you feel certain no one attends. And across
> the street, the railroad station. Most of all, that desolate
> feeling you get, young hunger, on a gray Sunday afternoon,
> when you survive only because the desolation feeds
> your dying, a dream of living alone on the edge
> of a definite place, a desert or the final house in town
> with no threat of expansion, or on the edge of a canyon,
> coyotes prowling below and a wind that never dies. . . .
> (from "Letter to Scanlon from Whitehall," 302)

The trick, of course, is to move the sheer welter of surface detail to epiphany, to make quotidian realities shimmer with transcendence. Not surprisingly, this is the leap that Hugo's imitators cannot make.

The letter poems were a way of "having it out," of saying plainly, and without apparent artifice, what needed to be said. A lyric poem, Hugo tells us, would not have done the trick. Of the group, the letter to Denise Levertov remained Hugo's favorite. Its controlling metaphors are economic ("This is the town where you choose sides / to die on, company or man, and both are losers.") and, one hastens to add, deeply divided:

> I have ambiguous feelings coming from a place like this
> and having clawed my way away, thanks to a few weak gifts
> and psychiatry and the luck of living in a country
> where enough money floats to the top for the shipwrecked
> to hang on. On one hand, no matter what my salary is
> or title, I remain a common laborer, stained by the perpetual
> dust from loading flour or coal. I stay humble, inadequate
> inside. . . .
>
> (308)

The slightest slip in tone and Hugo would have lost us midpoint. After all, this is not a poem in the "I-know-just-how-that-feels" school. Rather, it takes much greater risks—namely, first to surprise us (one does not normally imagine a full professor, and a distinguished poet to boot, making such a spectacle of his commonness) and then to convince us that the claims are true. "Letter to Levertov from Butte" *convinces*, especially as the latter half of the poem splits itself into a heart that goes out to

> . . . the wife who has turned
> forever to the wall, the husband sobbing at the kitchen
> table and the unwashed children taking it in and in and in
> until they are the wall, the table, even the dog the parents
> kill each month when the money's gone. . . .
>
> (308)

and the head that takes into full account of what lies on poverty's "other hand":

> I know the cruelty of poverty, the embittering ways
> love is denied, and food, the mean near-insanity of being
> and being deprived, the trivial compensations of each day,
> recapturing old years in broadcast tunes you try to recall
> in bars, hunched over the beer you can't afford, or bending
> to the bad job you're lucky enough to have. How, finally,
> hate takes over. . . .
>
> (308)

Nowhere, I would submit, are the alternating currents of Hugo's sensibility—its sympathies as well as its repulsions—more finely balanced. In this sense "Letter to Levertov from Butte" is to society what "Degrees of Gray in Philipsburg" is to triggering towns. And as in that earlier poem, Hugo cannot *not* take note of the fact that his lot is to define himself "apart" from the things that force him to say: "I don't want / to be part of it."

If there is empathy, even identification; if there is disgust bordering on hatred, they must, finally, find their expression in the life a poet leads and the words he makes into poems:

> . . . I want to be what I am, a writer good enough
> to teach with you and Gold and Singer, even if only in
> some conference leader's imagination. And I want my life
> inside to go on long as I do, though I only populate bare
> landscape with surrogate suffering, with lame men
> crippled by more than disease, and create finally
> a simple grief I can deal with, a pain the indigent can find
> acceptable. . . .
>
> (308)

These final lines point toward recovery, toward an end to the dark time *31 Letters and 13 Dreams* records, but it is, I think, more than that. Contemporary poets have a way of turning such material into a therapy of convention. They wax too shrill about their woe, and then too insistent about their recuperation. By contrast, the very modesty of Hugo's "wish" smacks of prayer, of psalm-making. In a poet as tough-minded about fundamentalism as he was, this is a remarkable, although hardly surprising, turn.

Hugo would, of course, deny he had gone so soft. He preferred the dream poems, for their "wildness," for the ways they approximated the rapid-fire transitions of an actual dream. In fact, when an interviewer asked Hugo if he could "analyze these dreams," he burst into laughter and replied, "Yes, I could analyze them. I think they're written for psychiatrists."

Behind Hugo's playful remark, however, lurks a thinly disguised truth—namely, that the dream poems are delimited by psychoanalysis, by the ways in which images tend to meet expectation and the formulaic replaces the genuinely experimental. If Hugo feared he had "forced" too many of the letter poems, one could argue that too many of the dream poems forced him. Consider, for example, these lines from "In Your Big Dream":

> Enemy subs pop up on the sea. They shell
> the coast. You wave your hair in surrender.
> Only one man comes ashore, a small man.
> He refuses your terms. He says it's not your land.
> You whine. You beg him to take you prisoner.
> Bison stampede the plain. You climb a mountain
> leading seven men who look like you. They depend
> on you for their safety. You climb higher
> and higher until you are alone under a sun
> gone pale in altitude. You climb above birds
> and clouds. You are home in this atmosphere.
>
> (312)

No doubt these poems originated in actual dreams, in something of the same way that the letter poems began in a flurry of actual letter-writing. But the situations sound remarkably like those Hugo includes in an essay called "Assumptions":

Years ago I was wealthy and lived in a New York penthouse. I hired about twenty chorus girls from Las Vegas to move in with me. For a year they played out all my sexual fantasies. At the end of the year my money was gone. The chorus girls had no interest in me once I was poor and they returned to Las Vegas. I moved here where, destitute in a one-room shack on the edge of town, I am living my life out in shame.

One man is a social misfit. He is thrown out of bars and not allowed in church. He shuffles about the street unable to find work and is subjected to insults and disdainful remarks by beautiful girls. He tries to make friends but can't.

A man takes menial jobs for which he is paid very little. He is grateful for what little work he can find and is always cheerful. In any encounter with others he assumes he is wrong and backs down. His place in the town social structure is assured. (*TT*, 22–23)

Behind each of the scenarios—be they "dream" or assumption—lies an aspect of Hugo. Which is to say, about some breakdowns there is little surprise.

But in Hugo's case, if there was a relentless honesty of emotion, there was also a saving sense of humor. Not *all* the dreams were self-lacerating, scary, or dripping with despair. As "In Your Good Dream" would have it:

> . . . All day festive tunes
> explain your problems are over. You picnic
> alone on clean lawn with your legend.
> Girls won't make fun of you here. . . .

> You know they are happy. Best to stay
> on the hill, drowsy witness, hearing
> the music, seeing their faces beam
> and knowing they marry forever, die late
> and are honored in death. A local process,
> no patent applied for, cuts name, born date
> and died too deep in the headstone to blur.
> (319)

Perhaps the line from "Letter to Kathy from Wisdom" says it best: "Until we die our lives are on the mend." One felt that mending process as *31 Letters and 13 Dreams* moved toward its concluding poems, and even more strongly in Hugo's last books: *White Center* (1980) and *The Right Madness on Skye* (1980). In the title poem of *White Center,* for example, he makes an imaginative return to the scenes of his childhood, those multiple indignations that fueled his earliest poems. But this time, perspective makes for significant differences:

> . . . I hoped forty years
> I'd write and would not write this poem. This town would die
> and your grave never reopen. Or mine. Because I'm married
> and happy, and across the street a foster child
> from a cruel past is safe and need no longer crawl
> for his meals, I walk this past with you, ghost in any field
> of good crops, certain I remember everything wrong.
> If not, why is this road lined thick with fern
> and why do I feel no shame kicking the loose gravel home?
>
> (375)

If Hugo's lines are more open, his language more immediate and precisely telling, it is also true that the ambiguities (does the speaker protest too much about his lack of shame?) become more subtle, more deeply felt. Playfulness finds a place—not merely as a function of a poet's love affair with language (no small matter, to be sure), but also as a way of echoing Whitman's "Have you practis'd so long to learn to read? / Have you felt so proud to get at the meaning of poems?" in our own time. As Hugo puts it:

> You think you've got it? Forget it. That young strong man
> I dreamed was not me. The old man had more than one day
> of fun. Some good weather repeats. He was more proud than
>   my dream credits him and he was less sad
> than whiskey might make him seem. Besides, when old
> no matter how sharp you may limp in some child's crippled
>   eye.
>
> (341)

"Leaving the Dream" suggests a jocose-serious response to those earlier dream poems that had found their genesis in Hugo's psychoanalysis. To dream the dream of an old man, "drunk and alone," is to comment on aspects of Hugo himself here reflected in the dream of a second man "younger than him / and strong poking fun when the old one fell in the dirt," who is yet another of Hugo's mirror images. Sometimes good weather repeats itself; Hugo might well have insisted otherwise thirty years earlier. And sometimes people outlive, sometimes even transcend, their pain.

White Center is an effort to "take possession"—of one's past, of one's landscape, of one's life—by acts of love that are inextricably connected to acts of language. As "A Good View From Flagstaff" puts it, in tones that add a measure of accommodation, of *acceptance,* to Hugo's more familiar stance:

> A good view here. We ignore the mean acts
> in the houses though we can't forget they go on
> daily with the soul's attrition. . . . Spread the way it is
> by wind, the world in cultivated patchwork
> claims we travel on the right freight one day
> and the years are gone. At worst
> they're more than nothing. The best friends
> we remember took us home the way we are.
>
> (351)

However much the final lines may echo Frost's sentiment about home as a place where "they have to take you in," what strikes me as more important is the gradually closing gap between what one insists on being and what one actually is.

No doubt Hugo's new wife and stepchildren played significant roles in this rehabilitation, this ability to let go of the self-lacerating, unappeasable parts of his personality. Not that Hugo's essential conservatism disappeared altogether: as he puts it in "Changes at Meridian": "One poet said it is enough to live perpetually in change. / He didn't believe it. I say we want everything static, / including farms we lose and rebuild" (357).

But love changed Hugo, made a poem like "With Melissa on the Shore" possible. There, in lines that remind us of Yeats's "A Prayer for my Daughter," Hugo means to teach his "sudden daughter"—this delicious piece of luck popped into his adult life—what his version of the Pacific Northwest signifies, how it shapes the contours of who he is, and how he writes:

> . . . Listen. The pound. Here
> we face our failure, words we should have said,
> anger that spilled over last Tuesday (you don't
> remember), the beggar we should have asked in.

The sea is fond of saying that's nothing.
Waves caving on sand say Melissa. The world makes demands
at impossible times and goes on burning with thirst.

(330–31)

A version of this same hard-earned love infuses *The Right Madness on Skye,* a volume that has both nothing—and everything—to do with Hugo's triggering northwestern landscape. One could argue that the isle of Skye (located off Scotland's coast) is worlds apart from the more familiar terrain of White Center, of Seattle, of Montana. Hugo comes to Skye bearing Guggenheim Foundation dollars and little else—no preconceptions, no especial hang-ups, no axes awaiting their poetic grindstone. In this regard, he meets the landscape and its people in ways markedly different from, say, Theodore Roethke's forays into the hard-drinking Ireland of his imagination.

But that much said, it is equally true that landscapes have a way of repeating themselves, and often in ways history usually doesn't. As Hugo points out in "Letter to Garber from Skye":

. . . It's windy nearly
all the time, and when you look out the window you think
it's cold. You go out and it isn't. The people too are like that.
Warmer than you think on first sight, with no throw-away charm
like in cities. The sky, water, vegetation and wind are Seattle.
The panoramic bare landscape's Montana. For me, two
homes in one.

(413–44)

The title poem adds that ultimate mutability called death to the mix. In giving wry, self-conscious instructions for his funeral "The Right Madness on Skye" reminds us of William Carlos Williams's "Tract." Like Williams, Hugo is out to teach his fellow townspeople how to conduct a funeral–partly by turning the usual conventions on their heads, partly by debunking death's mystery. But whereas Williams parodies both the tract and the etiquette book as he comments on the proper hearse-and-flowers for the dead person, Hugo turns the focus inward, not only to his burial, but also to a playful account of his shortcomings:

Alive, I often wounded my knee begging response.
My turn to put out. I will one eye to the blind of Dunvegan.
I will one ear to deaf salmon climbing the Conon.

And to the mute ocean I leave this haphazard tongue.
You might note on my stone in small letters:
Here lies one who believed all others his betters.
I didn't really, but what a fun thing to say.
And it's fun to be dead with one eye open in case
that stuck-up twitch in Arizona mourns my loss.

(417)

And yet, beyond the fun of Hugo's playful "confession" lie intimations of what a "right madness" might be and, to our retrospective ears, echoes of the death that would, in fact, strike Hugo down two years later. As our age would have it, there is madness, and madness. To celebrate one's death with music, with dance, and, most of all, with imagination is madness right-headed:

Come on, admit it—that blue tone I faked on my skin—
these eyes I kept closed tight in this poem.
Here's the right madness on Skye. Take five days
for piper and drum and tell the oxen, start dancing.
Mail Harry of Nothingham home to his nothing.
Take my word. It's been fun.

(419)

In "The Far Field" Theodore Roethke journeys to death's interior and discovers that he has

learned not to fear infinity:
The far field, the windy cliffs of forever:
The dying of time in the white light of tomorrow,
The wheel turning away from itself,
The sprawl of the wave,
The on-coming water.[17]

Hugo's last poems share much with those of his mentor; he, too, found a way to beat the Death Question.

Even more important perhaps, one felt that, in describing the happiness that Theodore Roethke and T. S. Eliot found late in their careers, Hugo was also talking—in sotto voce—about himself:

I remember I was distrustful of both Eliot and Roethke when late in their careers they announced they were happy. But they were being honest. Every poem a poet writes is a slight advance of self and a slight modification of the mask, the one you want to be. Poem after poem the self grows more worthy of the mask, the mask comes closer to fitting the face. After enough poems, you are nearly the one you want to be, and the one you want to be closely resembles you. (*TT*, 73–74)

Alas, death cheated Hugo out of a late career and the happiness we would like to imagine accompanying it. He died, a victim of leukemia, on 22 October 1982, at age fifty-eight. Of what generally passes for "accomplishments," there were many: his books had twice been nominated for National Book Awards; he won a Guggenheim Fellowship, a Rockefeller grant, and in 1979 the American Academy of Poets awarded him a ten-thousand-dollar fellowship "for distinguished poetic achievement"; he was judge of the Yale Younger Poets Series and head of the creative writing department at the University of Montana. Hugo was, in short, a major American poet.

What the obituaries leave out, however, is that Hugo was poetry's champion at a time when contemporary American poetry needed one. His lively readings brought a full measure of excitement to a wide variety of college campuses, and his dedicated teaching made a genuine difference to hundreds of his students. But I suspect he would prefer a more modest assessment of what his life's work came to—something, perhaps, like this "statement from faith" from *The Triggering Town*: "An act of imagination is an act of self-acceptance." Hugo gave us a great many such "acts" during his prolific public life; they changed our sense of what regionalism at its best can be and helped to strengthen the Pacific Northwest's contribution to our national literature. But most of all, I think, his poetry helped us to accept ourselves, and each other. That, rather than the bald recitation of facts, is the truest obituary.

DAVID WAGONER
(1922)
Photography by William Stafford

Chapter Four
David Wagoner:
Poetic Magic in the
Pacific Northwest

Biographical Sketch

David (Russell) Wagoner was born 5 June 1926 in Massillon, Ohio, a small town renowned largely for its high school football teams. He was raised in Whiting, Indiana, and educated at the George Rogers Clark High School of Hammond, Indiana. If there is always a truth that lies just beneath comic exaggerations, Wagoner's poem "A Valedictory to Standard Oil" tells us much about the gestalt of those times, that place.

From 1944 to 1946 Wagoner was a midshipman in the NROTC at Pennsylvania State University, where he received his A.B. in 1946. He continued his studies at Indiana University, completing his M.A. in 1949.

He spent the academic year 1949–50 at DePauw University, where he was an instructor in English. The following year he married Elizabeth Arensman and returned to Pennsylvania State University as an instructor.

Nineteen fifty-three was a significant year on several counts: Wagoner completed his stint at Pennsylvania State University and prepared to move west, to the University of Washington where he would join his mentor, Theodore Roethke; his marriage to Elizabeth Arensman ended in divorce; and he published his first collection of poetry, *Dry Sun, Dry Wind*.

Wagoner may be best known as a poet, but he has had a parallel career as a novelist, one that began in 1954 with the publication of *The Man in the Middle*. That novel was followed by *Money Money Money* in 1953 and a Guggenheim Fellowship in Fiction in 1956. Wagoner traveled to Spain, France, and England, presumably taking the tragicomic vision of his fiction with him.

Wagoner the poet and Wagoner the fictionist were both repre-
sented in 1958, with the publications of *Rock,* a novel, and *A Place
to Stand,* a collection of poems. In 1961 he married Patricia Lee
Parrott, the muse behind the making of poems like "A Guide to
Dungeness Spit." He published yet another collection of poems, *The
Nesting Ground,* in 1963.

In 1964 he tried his hand at drama, as a Ford Fellow in Drama.
He worked closely with the Seattle Repertory Theatre as their playwright in residence. If the result did not lure him out of the English
Department or away from his writing desk where he continued to
write poetry and novels, it did lead to a number of dramatic pieces
that found their way into subsequent collections of his poetry.

The Escape Artist, probably Wagoner's best-known novel, was published in 1965. After many delays, a film version, produced by Francis Ford Coppola, was released in 1982. Wagoner had high hopes for
its success, but the film collected only modest reviews and did medio-
cre business at the box office.

By contrast, his poetry thrived, and his reputation grew steadily.
For many critics, *Staying Alive,* published in 1966, was the watershed
book. In the same year he became editor of *Poetry Northwest* and the
rest, as they say, is history. During the following year Wagoner won
the Zabel Prize from *Poetry* (Chicago) and an award from the National
Institute of Arts and Letters. He was, by any reckoning, a significant,
if not a major, poet.

In 1968 he was the Elliston Lecturer in Modern Poetry at the Uni-
versity of Cincinnati and, a year later, he published *New and Selected
Poems.* During the same year he won a National Council on the Arts
Award.

Lest one feel that all this might make Wagoner neglect his fiction,
he published *Where is My Wandering Boy Tonight?* in 1970. In 1971
he did a reading/lecture tour for the U.S. Information Agency in
Greece, Turkey, and Lebanon.

Wagoner combined his talent as a poet and his growing skills as
an editor in 1972, publishing two books, one a collection of poetry
(Riverbed) and the other a selection from Theodore Roethke's notebooks entitled *Straw for the Fire.*

During the following year Wagoner published yet another collection of poetry, *Sleeping in the Woods,* and won the Blumenthal-
Leviton-Blonder Prize from *Poetry* (Chicago).

The prizes continued. In 1975 he won *two* Fels Prizes from the Coordinating Council of Literary Magazines, one for poetry, the other for editing.

His *Collected Poems, 1956–1976* appeared in 1976. The volume makes his achievement as a poet clear, not only in terms of sheer production, but also with regard to consistent quality. Indeed, it would be difficult to think of a twenty-year span in any other living American poet that could equal Wagoner's accomplishment.

The poetic establishment clearly agreed. In 1977 Wagoner won a Pushcart Prize in poetry, the Tietjens Prize from *Poetry* (Chicago), and he was nominated for a National Book Award in poetry. The following year he was elected one of the twelve chancellors of the Academy of American Poets and was named editor of the Princeton University Press Contemporary Poetry Series. Not surprisingly, he also published a new volume of poetry, *Who Shall be the Sun?*

The awards continued. In 1970 Wagoner published *In Broken Country* and in that same year was given the Pacific Northwest Booksellers Award for Excellence in Writing. In 1980 he was nominated for the American Book Award in poetry and he received a Sherwood Anderson Award in fiction. He also received the English-speaking Union Prize from *Poetry* (Chicago). That same year he published another work of fiction, *The Hanging Garden.*

Landfall, a collection of poems, was published in 1981. The following year he divorced Patricia Lee Parrott, his wife of twenty-one years, and married Robin Heather Seyfried.

In 1983 Wagoner won yet another Pushcart Prize in poetry and became editor of the University of Missouri Press Breakthrough Series. He also pubished another collection of his own poems entitled *First Light.*

In 1985 he won the Charles Angoff Prize from the *Literary Review.* Books and prizes, prizes and books—in either combination, the phrase describes Wagoner's rich, varied, and altogether astounding career. That it will continue apace is, by this time, a safe bet; that it will continue to develop, to grow, is even safer.

Themes and Techniques

> "Wind, bird, and tree,
> Water, grass, and light:
> In half of what I write . . .
> The same six words recur."
> —from Wagoner's
> "The Words"[1]

The time was early September 1963; the place, Parrington Hall on the University of Washington campus. Theodore Roethke had died of a heart attack in a swank, private swimming pool the month before— a victim, presumably, of the manic energy, the voraciousness, that made him swim more laps than a man his age should have, and that had energized his best poems.

The university was in mourning in the predictable ways an academic institution mourns the loss of its poet in residence: every scrap of paper from his desk and filing cabinet was spirited off in cardboard boxes to the Library; over coffee, plans were hatched about possible replacements, with the sharp-eyed determination and often the relish of a horse swap; the nameplate over his office door mysteriously disappeared; the more ambitious drifted off to sleep as visions of an essay— or perchance a book—about Roethke danced through their heads. In short, the modification from teacher and collegue to Major Poet had begun.

If Roethke were only a small part of what, in those days, I thought of as my raison d'être, he was, at least, my reason for being at the University of Washington. I had come there as a graduate teaching assistant, mightily impressed with his poems—or at least as impressed as one can be after an undergraduate Contemporary American Poetry course and a term paper devoted to his work—and hoping to land a spot in his verse-writing seminar. Instead, Death cheated me, gave me a "film" of Roethke ["In a Dark Time"] instead. The room was packed with people who had been in his classroom, who had been to his readings, who had been to his parties, who knew the Roethke apocrypha firsthand. But before the lights were lowered and Roethke's voice would fill up the eerie silence of that fall afternoon, a member of the English Department rose to make what usually travels under the banner of "a few appropriate remarks." He was awkward, obviously ill at ease. His voice choked at the beginning, cracked in spots throughout. And yet his words were as unforgettable as he was. I am speaking, of course, about David Wagoner.

To be sure, Wagoner did not use the occasion to rehearse the nearly twenty-year span during which he had been Roethke's student (at Penn State University) and, since 1954, his colleague at the University of Washington. Rather, Wagoner compressed a world of complex emotions into a few articulate paragraphs. I remembered thinking to myself, at my flippant worst, that a poet had no business being so handsome. He wore his clothes *too* well, coiffed his hair a touch *too* much, carried himself too much like the peacock. He was, in short, Narcissus's fair-haired boy.

It was easy to imagine him chucking the art business and making a tidy living as a male model, probably for cigarette ads or high-priced cars. I was, of course, both uncharitable and dead wrong, although, some twenty years later, journalists in the Northwest still write about Wagoner as if he were just another "pretty face" (e.g., "At 54, Wagoner is as tan, trim and polished-looking as a Beverly Hills tennis pro. He wears rose-colored glasses. His hair is silver and his eyebrows black.").

And yet, my introduction to Wagoner may not have been uncharacteristic after all. He remains, in large measure, shy, even hesitant, his eyes tending to dart around the periphery of a conversation as if he were a stalked animal. And this is especially true when he begins to feel the hot breath of a critical label on the back of his neck. As he put it in a letter:

I have no idea what a Northwest poet is. If you want to talk about that in your book, you're on your own. . . . [Also] I think the Roethke connection is getting pretty remote by now."[2]

Wagoner is "right," of course—that is, in the ways poets always, and rightfully, squirm when they see themselves being herded toward the pigeonholes of convenience. After all, he is now older than Roethke was when he died and he has, by dint of years of hard, consistent work, made a wide variety of subjects and techniques his own. That the linkages persist is, I suppose, a function of how we write the history of contemporary American poets (X studied with Y at the University of Z) and the place an established poet chooses to work. As a young poet Wagoner "chose" Roethke, with all the assets and the liabilities that went with such a choice, and as a man in his late fifties, he had chosen to remain in the Pacific Northwest—teaching at the University of Washington, editing *Poetry Northwest,* laying himself wide open for the label "Northwest poet." Granted, the adjective may hang around his neck (or perhaps, stick in his craw) like an added, unnecessary weight—*poet* being a sufficient description/definition of what he is, what he *does*—but it should hardly strike him as a surprise. Wagoner, in short, has been associated with the Pacific Northwest too long, not only in terms of where he lives but, more important, in terms of what he writes about.

Several years ago I wrote the following introductory paragraph to a piece about Wagoner:

Since, roughly, the end of the Second World War America has been blessed with any number of accomplished poets. But none seems more consistently satisfying than David Wagoner. At the present moment both the shrill sounds of the public poet and the equally shrill sounds of the confessionally private one have escalated to the point of diminishing returns. Which is to say, the social tragedies which surround us—whether they be a lingering war in Vietnam, the ongoing racial agony or man's regular inhumanity to man—have a way of depleting the poetic arsenal without ever quite achieving the desired effect. Perhaps our headlines are too monstrous for *any* poem, even one recited with passion to an audience willing to respond with appropriate indignation. On more personal fronts, the race to confess some "horrible" truth leads to exhaustion, if not the conventionally boring. With no-holds barred—and a society that has made a shambles of restraint—perhaps the only shocking revelation left to tell is that one is (1) heterosexual (2) happily married, on the whole (3) not particularly fucked up. Such a poet may yet appear—and he may even refuse to appear in lime-colored flares and moppish hair—but it is hard to buck a tradition which expects our poets to "come on strong."[3]

Much has changed since the days when confessional poets ruled the poetic roost, when romantic lives counted for more than disciplined work, when a word like *style* found itself tacked onto a word like *life*. We no longer insist that our poets be young to be trusted, or be militant to be politically engagé.

Nonetheless, certain suspicions about the comfortably middle-aged remain. Robert Peters, a poet/critic who pushes the iconoclastic until it becomes the merely cranky, puts it this way:

What is David Wagoner's poetry like? Little Brown [Wagoner's publisher] touts it as "timeless and arresting." Let's have a close look at this blackbird of American verse as he wings through the air. . . . Wagoner reflects a middle-class sensibility as that sensibility approaches middle age. His emotional reponses fall within the framework of the entirely possible, non-controversial, and secure. He falls asleep in gardens, he stands around in swamps and in woods and on lake shores, and he evokes the fairly pleasant circumstances of a calm, productive, and pleasant existence. . . . Life, one feels, has been pretty good to him; and his meditations on man and nature evolve from a nicely fixed center. . . . His imagination is largely a domestic one: he never seems far from home. He's seldom off a moderately well-beaten path.[4]

In short, Wagoner is no Huck Finn, and Peters takes some pains to make him pay for it. But how telling—to say nothing of "fair"—are the accusations? Is Wagoner as placid, as safe, as Peters suggests?

Certainly Peters cannot have in mind a poem like "To My Friend Whose Parachute Did Not Open" (the opening selection of *Collected Poems,* taken from Wagoner's first book, *A Place to Stand* [1958]). For there Wagoner juxtaposes the need to find a "place to stand," a poetic space of his own, against his friend's terrible fall:

> Down the smooth slope of your trajectory,
> Obeying physics like a bauble of hail,
> Thirty-two feet per second hurled
> Toward treetops, cows, and crouching gravity
> From the unreasonable center of the world.

Like all elegies, this is a poem as much about its speaker as about its presumed subject. It is also a poem about its own making:

> You outraced thought. What good was thinking then? . . .
> I know angelic wisdom leaped from your mouth,
> But not in words, for words can be afraid:
>
> You sang a paean at the speed of sound,
> Compressed miraculous air within your head
> And made it fountain upward like a cowl.
> And if you didn't, then you struck the ground.
> And if you struck the ground, both of us died.
>
> (3)

Self-conscious? Perhaps, but certainly not *safe,* for Wagoner manages to infuse the very act of writing with a concretely rendered sense of terror.

One could argue, of course, that "To My Friend . . ." is not representative of the later, more mature Wagoner. In this sense a poem like "Murder Mystery" would, no doubt, strike Peters as a better choice. It is full of the comic highjinks and parodic spirit we have learned to associate with Wagoner's poetry. The impulse toward exaggeration and "send-up" showed itself early—in this case, as a version of Agatha Christie turned on its head:

> After the murder, like parades of Fools,
> The bungling supernumeraries come,
> Sniffing at footprints, looking under rugs,
> Clasping the dead man with prehensile tools.
> Lens against nose, false beard down to his knees,
> The Hawkshaw enters, hoists his bag of tricks,
> And passes out suspicion like lemonade . . .
>   (10)

Among Wagoner's continuing strengths in his sense of the dramatic, the ways in which Wagoner the novelist (e.g., *Where is My Wandering Boy Tonight?' The Road to Many a Wonder, The Escape Artist*) cross-fertilizes Wagoner the poet. Granted, there are times when too much suspicion is too glibly passed around "like lemonade," but that is simply by way of saying that Wagoner is hardly as safe or as predictable a poet as Peters would have him be.

A Place to Stand was an impressive debut, but it was "A Guide to Dungeness Spit" from Wagoner's third collection, *The Nesting Ground* (1963), that made him a poet. Unlike, say, "Murder Mystery," this was a poem that had its origins and its exact details in direct experience. It is also a poem in the instructional mode, but one that splits the speaker's voice between a lecturer who is "guiding" us, showing us how-to-see this tiny piece of northwestern turf, and our growing sense that this is also the voice of somebody falling deeply in love with the "other" of the poem:

> Those are tears. Those are called houses, and those are people.
> Here is a stairway past the whites of our eyes.
> All our distance
> Has ended in the light. We climb to the light in spirals,
> And look, between us we have come all the way,
> And it never ends
> In the ocean, the spit and image of our guided travels.
> Those are called ships. We are called lovers.
> There lie the mountains.
>   (20)

Wagoner was, of course, talking about the Patt Parrott who, shortly after the poem was written, became his wife.

Interestingly enough, the bulk of the poem was written on the back of a manila envelope while Wagoner was proctoring a final examination at the University of Washington. Granted, he made additions and some changes later, but he insists that the poem essentially composed itself. Or, more correctly, it seemed to, for behind "A Guide to Dungeness Spit" lie models like William Carlos Williams's "Tract" ("I will teach you, my townspeople / how to perform a funeral") and Henry Reed's "Judging Distances"; echoes from D. H. Lawrence (e.g., "we have come all the way") and Theodore Roethke. The result gave this early—and I think, remarkable—poem the heft, the *feel,* of an oblique modernist posture.

Still, the instructional mode of "A Guide to Dungeness Spit" has served Wagoner well. If the impulse to break into "lecture" rather than song is one of the academic poet's liabilities, Wagoner has turned the orderly recitation of particulars into a decided asset. In short, he writes dramatic monologues that remind us of Browning much more than they do of Wagoner's immediate predecessors. The form—generally that of a veteran giving instruction to a novice—becomes a lively way to generate elegant wit and darker wisdoms that the solidly cheerful views of Wagoner generally allow for.

In the years since "A Guide to Dungeness Spit" Wagoner has written a series of these instructional poems, including "Staying Alive" ("Staying alive in the woods is a matter of calming down"), "Police Manual," "The Shooting Lesson" ("Our aim should be the aim / Of a lifetime, all our habits rolled into one"), and others. There was a time, he confessed to me recently, when he worried about repeating himself, even about self-parody, but the dream of complete breaks with one's poetic past, of quantum leaps into the Entirely New, is (he concluded) something of a mug's game. By W.H. Auden's measure—that one should easily be able to tell a poet's early work from his "middle period," and both from his mature efforts—Wagoner is not at all impressive. There are, however, other benchmarks one might apply—consistency, for example, or simply the accumulated weight of one's oeuvre—and seen in those lights, Wagoner need not apologize for making the instructional voice his own. After all, nobody criticizes composers or painters for working out variations on a theme.

In Wagoner's case, both the magic that life presents to him, and
the patterning he brings to the process of making it art, are found in
themes that keep recurring. Poems of instruction are merely one example. Like his special fondness for beginning titles with a gerund
(e.g., "Walking in the Snow"; "Looking for Mountain Beavers";
"Staying Alive"), Wagoner seeks out that edge where noun and verb
intersect, where an explaining (lecturing?) voice can unfold the drama
at an arm's length. One suspects that this distancing is somehow re-
lated to his shyness, to a certain coolness in his demeanor. When he
was a young boy, magic tricks were an attention-grabbing, crowd-
pleasing way of overcoming this reticence; in this regard, what attracted him to illusion, to sleight of hand, is precisely the same thing
that appealed to, say, the young Johnny Carson (another shy, midwestern lad) and hundreds of other would-be Blackstones.

In Wagoner's case, however, the original impulse transmogrified
itself into dazzling diction and an elegant wit. Like the magician, the
poem's voice controls the situation and its reality. Language is, in
this sense, the "inexhaustible hat" out of which all manner of rabbits
pop:

> The incomparable Monsieur Hartz in 1880
> . . . produced from a borrowed hat
> Seven glass lanterns, each with a lighted candle.
> A swaddle of scarves, hundreds of yards of bunting,
> A lady's bustle, a stack of empty boxes,
> A cage with a lovely, stuffed, half-cocked canary . . .
> And lastly a grinning skull.
> (from "The Inexhaustible Hat," 151)

The concrete details about Monsieur Hartz are as "correct" as they are
precise. I belabor this matter partly because Wagoner's wide-ranging,
often quirky, reading generates many of his poems; partly because
this inclination toward the bookish, the cerebral, establishes the aesthetic distance he apparently requires.

In a shrewd, often telling review of Wagoner's *In Broken Country*
(1979) Richard Hugo pays an elaborate compliment to the elegantly
"Elizabethan" quality of the verse, but then goes on to suggest, with
some left-handed "praise," the lines of essential difference between
Wagner and himself, as well as between Wagoner and other more
typically northwestern poets:

. . . The rest of us pursue that elusive quality we call "voice" in our poems, assuming somewhere we find one that is ours. We write as if our vocabularies of necessity are limited. We use few words that aren't relegated by the social forces of democracy to common use. When we talk (write) the utterance itself has to be accepted and believed. At our best our ancestors go back no farther than the 17th century, and they came down to us often filtered through those who immediately preceded us. Often our ancestors are but one genera-tion removed, not really ancestors at all, but there just the same. [By con-trast] David Wagoner has always written as if for him, as for the Elizabethans, the language is a recent development. The world and words are new, ready to be explored for possibilities, ready for discovery's rewarding delights. His "voice," the speaker in or behind the poem, had seemed sec-ondary to the wonder of what each poem could locate for its use, both vocab-ulary and images.[5]

Among the many wise things T. S. Eliot has taught us is the unsur-prising fact that poets tend to talk about themselves when they talk about others—either by way of justifying work already done or, more interestingly, to clarify their own work-in-progress. This is clearly the case with Hugo on Wagoner—although it is also a case of hitting the nail dead center. What makes Wagoner's "voice" so elusive, so hard to locate, is precisely this strain of Elizabethan wit.

Consider, for example, a seriocomic narrative like "The Shooting of John Dillinger Outside the Biograph Theatre, July 22, 1934," a poem that, on first glance, seems very far indeed from either the Eliz-abethan world or its sense of wit. And yet, the very title suggests the overloading of "fact" that will operate throughout:

Chicago ran a fever of a hundred and one that groggy Sunday.
A reporter fried an egg on a sidewalk; the air looked shaky.
And a hundred thousand people were in the lake like shirts in a laundry.
Why was Johnny lonely?

(59)

In public readings Wagoner milks the slant rhymes (shaky/laundry/ lonely) until they turn to butter; that he sustains the slightly "off" rhymes for nearly one hundred, elongated lines is, of course, part of the verbal fun. So too, is the accuracy of his indefatigable "research":

Was Johnny a thinker?
No, but he was thinking more or less of Billie Frechette

Who was lost in prison for longer than he could possibly wait.
And then it was suddenly too hard to think around a bullet.
Did anyone shoot straight?
Yes, but Mrs. Etta Natalsky fell out from under her picture hat.
Theresa Paulus sprawled on the sidewalk, clutching her left foot.
And both of them groaned loud and long under the streetlight.
Did Johnny like that?

(60–61)

One could argue that the repetitions generated by the poem's structure of questions-and-answers creates the effect of litany, or even, I suppose, that it has something of the Joycean flavor of the "Ithaca" chapter in *Ulysses*. But I prefer to see the playfulness as a reflection of Wagoner's more general self-consciousness about poetry. Retelling the "facts" that surrounded Dillinger's death not only allowed for puns of the middle water (". . . the minister said, 'With luck, he could have been a minister.' / And up the sleeve of his oversized gray suit, Johnny twitched a finger."), but also some sardonic commentary on what fame—political or poetic—comes to in the Midwest:

> . . . They planted him [Dillinger] in a
>   cemetery
> With three unknown vice presidents, Benjamin
>   Harrison, and James Whitcomb Riley,
> Who never held up anybody.

(62)

The theme continues—this time clustered around the image of the poet-as-bullfrog—in "The Poets Agree to be Quiet by the Swamp" ("They stick their elbows out into the evening, / Stoop, and begin the ancient croaking."); in "Revival" (where Wagoner imagines himself and Richard Hugo as numbered among those who "can't keep out of lovers' lane for a minute, / Who, when they trip, will lie there in the rut / For old time's sake, rebellious as all Hell, / Croaking forever, loving the hard way."); and in literally dozens of Wagoner poems about the making of poems.

Nonetheless, *Staying Alive* (1966) represented an important breakthrough—into a congenial voice and a level of confidence that those more psychoanalytically inclined than I might well attribute to Roethke's death. That Wagoner wrote many of the poems while he was Roethke Professor (assuming the large shoes his mentor had left vacant when he died in 1963) smacks of yet another installment in the anxiety about influence mode. It is also more than a little simplistic, missing more of Wagner's essence than it hits. The plainer truth is that he ranks among our hardest-working, most prolific of contemporary poets. A typical Wagoner poem like "Going to Pieces" is an example of verbal wit and technical control polished to a high, dazzling relief. Here, the clichés about "falling apart" are systematically turned inside out, made to transcend their own banality:

> But looking around and seeing other people
> Coming apart at parties, breaking up
> And catching their own laughter in both hands.
> Or crossing the lawn and throwing up their spirits
> Like voice-balloons in funnies, touching noses
> In bedroom mirrors, one after another,
> I figure something can be said for it:
> Maybe some people break in better halves
> Or some of the parts are greater than the whole.
>
> (73)

In the "Dillinger" poem Wagoner works slant rhymes for all they are worth; here, he pays attention to the effects that line breaks—especially those words positioned on the far right—can create. But the poem is more, much more, than clever puns about "spirits" thrown up or the gerunds that have become something of a Wagoner trademark. Rather, it is his ability to sustain a central metaphor, to work it through the poem like a spine, that makes "Going to Pieces" fit so satisfactorily on a magazine page. Here, for example, is what happens when a hypothesis about marionette-show skeletons merges with Wagoner's observation of people "coming apart" at parties to create an intriguing syllogism/image, courtesy of the palolo worm:

> Now I'll tell you one: the palolo worms,
> One night a year at the bottom of the sea,
> Back halfway out of the burrows where they spend
> Long lives; their tails turn luminous, twist free,
> And all by themselves swim up to the surface,
> Joining with millions of other detached tails;
> The sea in a writhing mass lies white for miles

Under a gibbous moon; the bright halves die
And float away like scraps after a party,
But leave behind their larvae, set for life.

(73)

Increasingly, too, Wagoner worked a northwestern landscape into
the fabric of his metaphor—not only with his abiding concern for anthropological detail (an interest that continues to dominate those collections published after *Collected Poems, 1956–1976*)—or in his nature
poems (e.g., "The soul goes straight away as the crow flies / With
enough noise to wake what's left behind / And leave it, one eye up,
like a dying salmon" ["Sleeping by a River"]), but also in poems that
are, finally, about the writing of poems:

The Osprey's Nest

The osprey's nest has dropped off its own weight
After years, breaking everything under it, collapsing
Out of the sky like the wreckage of the moon.
Having killed its branch and rotted its lodgepole:
A flying cloud of fishbones tall as a man
A shambles of dead storms ten feet across.

Uncertain what holds anything together,
Ospreys try everything—fishnets and broomsticks,
Welcome-mats and pieces of scarecrows,
Sheep bones, shells, the folded wings of mallards—
And heap up generations till they topple.

(87)

Let me hasten to add that Wagoner *knows* his ospreys, that he sees
and writes clearly about them. But what made *Staying Alive* so impressive was our sense of a voice merging with its external environment. With Hugo, the "triggering town" moved by increments
toward the confessional bone. By contrast, Wagoner preferred to play
out his risks against a backdrop of convention—experimenting with
forms, piling one brilliant verbal effect upon another.

At first glance *New and Selected Poems* (1969) looked like more of
the same. What worked with Dillinger's death could be reworked as
Coxey's March; Seattle's down-and-outers (e.g., "At St. Vincent
Depaul's" or "Bums at Breakfast") were always good for an instruc-

tive, sardonic lesson. But there was also a growing sense that his portraiture was drawn from the exotic, the underworld, the marginal.
"The Burglar," for example, opens with these lines:

> Being a burglar, you slip out of doors in the morning
> And look at the street by looking at the sky,
> Not being taken in by anything blue.
> You must look to the left or right to see across.
> If nothing strikes your eye, if no one comes running,
> You've stolen another day.
>
> (110)

Or these lines that conclude an account of "The Hold-Up":

> The muzzle touches my back
> Gently, like the muzzle of a dog. What's holding me up?
> Take off your shoes. I stand in stocking feet
> On the cinders. He begins to fade. . . .
> My shoes and my money are running away in the dark.
>
> (112)

With only a few exceptions (e.g., "Searching in the Britannia Tavern," with its dedication to Earl Lund of the Clallam Tribe and its
evocations of down-at-its-heels Indian mythology or "The Soles" lying
"in shallows off Dungeness Spit"), *New and Selected Poems* takes its in-
spiration from sources not tied to a specific landscape. Notions of
"soul"—everything from the enigmatic "Note from Body to Soul" to
"Blues to Be Sung in a Dark Voice"—suggest the meditative, rather
than the neat category of images Wagoner provided in his earlier
poem, "The Words." In this sense, one would be hard-pressed to
think of him as a northwestern poet in quite the same way that, say,
John Crowe Ransom was a distinctly "Southern" writer. True, there
are northwestern settings, even an integral connection with the land
and its animals (see, for example, "Nine Charms Against the
Hunter"), but Wagoner is simply too foxy, too much the "escape artist," if you will, to be bound by the straitjacket of a label.

Put another way, for all the northestern geography in poems like
"A Guide to Dungeness Spit," Wagoner has retained an ear condi-
tioned by the Midwest from which he came. His most characteristic
pitch is a flat, almost-wry combination of the matter-of-fact and the

mildly self-deprecating. It is a unique note in contemporary letters, for all the kinship to Hoosiers who have come before. Generally speaking, it manifests itself in a quiet astonishment, at once a reverence for the intrinsic magic that is life and a continual surprise as one encounters it again and again. The terms of the astonishment grow inevitably out of dramatic situations that prefer the landscape of actuality to the larger surfaces of unbridled dream. That is, Wagoner may occasionally pitch his material in the bizarre (as he does in "The Keepers" [from *River Bed,* 1972]) but whatever lines have been cast upon sensational waters hook back to that curious interaction between man and Nature that is his strongest suit.

Granted, Wagoner's playfulness suspends, at least temporarily, much of the seriousness I've been rather straining to point out. In "The Keepers," for example, the ambiguity of his title compounds the question of who, exactly, is keeping whom. On a day when "The drizzle and wind had driven the keepers / Indoors," the speaker and a woman observe the aquarium uneasily:

> We stood between the seals and the whale tank,
> Our games rained out like theirs.

> But she climbed to the round catwalk
> Ahead of me, and there was the sleek half-grown
> Black-and-white killer whale, being heaved
> And lapped by its own backwash.

What follows is a moment out of some half-forgotten chapter of human history, one that combines the Earth Mother with La Belle Dame Sans Merci, the face of Eve with the aspect of Lilith. As the killer whale swims his "flat circle," the woman calls out something the speaker cannot quite hear in the tearing wind that is the aquarium. The whale, however, evidently can; his tongue responds—sticking out from a huge head and perfectly pointed teeth—when suddenly:

> She kissed it, as God is my witness. The whale
> Sank back and swam as it had before.
> She came toward me at the top of the stair,
> As I braced against the wind blowing between us,

> And offered me those same lips to be kissed.
> And something I hadn't dared
> Believe in, something deep as my salt
> Rose to the surface of my mouth to touch them.
>
> (139)

In *Riverbed* the deepest yearnings are often couched in emotions that verge on surprise. Here, for example, both whale and man respond to primal needs with particularly primal gestures. Ultimately, even a sophisticated stance and the off-rhymes of a line like "She kissed it, as God is my witness" are subsumed by that which is more basic. Wagoner's tendency is to come at such moments from an oblique angle we recognize as wit, but the gentle sense of verbal play always teeters toward a transposed key, that "something I hadn't dared / Believe in." Moreover, the *something* "deep as my salt / Rose to the surface of my mouth to touch them."

At a time when "religious" poets are still measured by the more sensational yardstick of a conversion embraced or rejected, Wagoner's poetry speaks of a reverence for that subtle relationship between man and animal. It is this spirit that draws his characters to the spawning grounds of the relentless salmon in the collection's title poem:

> We come back to find them, to wait at their nesting hollows
> With the same unreasoning hope. . . .
>
> In a month of rain, the water will rise above
> Where we stand on a curving shelf below an island—
> The blue daylight scattered and the leaves
> All castaways like us for a season.
>
> (137)

The terrible cost of fertility is mirrored in the lovers who "lie down all day" beside the dying salmon, partaking of a ritual that lies between language and the surrounding landscape of flat rocks, swift-flowing streams.

A similar note is struck in "The Fisherman's Wife." Once again there is a doubling effect: the "wife" cradles a trout (freed by her objections, from the fisherman's hook) in much the same way that their instinctive response helps to nurture him. And yet, it is the fisherman who catches his wife "by the hair bringing her back alive" as she sinks into the lake on her mission of mercy. What begins in a ritualized death ends in an equally ritualized life: "We sat on edge till the moon came out, but nothing / Rose, belly up, to mock it at our feet."

As with the lovers of "In the Badlands," the tableau freezes motion at a point somewhere between accomplished dread and miraculous salvation. Overhead the vultures sail "With our love as the pivot"; a sea of fossils lies beneath them. But at this moment of precious equipoise—a time that calls to mind "Staying Alive"—suspended animation makes for the poetic possibility. In such poems death is warded off and the context is savored in its stead. And, too, there is a quiet astonishment about both the original predicament and one's response to its potential meaning. Love, of course, is the life-sustaining counter, but Wagoner's first, almost clinical, tone and the gentle contours of his ironic wit hold the gush of sentimentality at a necessary remove.

Very often his brand of secret sharing at the zoo reminds one of Rilke. In *Staying Alive* an extraordinary poem entitled "The Fruit of the Tree" focused on a curious pear and equally curious camel who gobbled it up through the bars. in "Waiting with the Snowy Owls" from *River Bed,* Wagoner balances the moment of communion between nine owls (presumably waiting for the sun to melt "What holds them, to run from them or stir / The thawed halves of hearts at their feet") and a similar condition mirrored in his inability to "read or write."

The difference, is that Wagoner "recovers" from his momentary block; indeed, "Waiting with the Snowy Owls" is Exhibit A. But there are other moments when the distance between poet and speaker dissolves, when we imagine him playing his hand "straight." A manifesto poem like "The Words" in *Staying Alive* begs to be taken literally, as the six keys that unlock Wagoner's poetic world. Granted, *wind, bird, tree, water, grass,* and *light* loom as important benchmarks, but one also suspects that Wagoner is having a bit of fun at his more dogged critics' expense. After all, there is nothing quite like beating "close readers" (especially those of the word-counting sort) to the punch. And yet, a *Wagoner Concordance*—when such an animal appears, as it surely must—is likely to prove otherwise, especially where the matter of his congenial themes is concerned. Since *New and Selected Poems,* magic has been a constant motif, one that fuses craft with astonishment, illusion with reality, the need to conceal with the urge to reveal. Unlike other contemporary poets, Wagoner neither plays at being the ersatz magician nor does he advertise himself as an incarnation of the shaman. Rather, he brings to "magic" something of the egg-in-tongue spirit of a poem like "The Extraordinary Production of Eggs from the Mouth in *Riverbed*." Versions of nothingness frame the poem, from its opening stanza in which the Professor/Magician

> Shows us he has nothing
> up his sleeve or under his coattails,
> Then lowers his brows as seriously as a man
> Thinking of being something else, and there,
> Would you believe it, from between his lips
> The white tip of an egg comes mooning out. . . .

to its final lines, where literally dozens of eggs find their way back to the mouth, the source, from whence they came:

> But now with a flick of the wrist, seeming to think
> Better of his wobbly bonewhite offspring,
> He puts one into his mouth, and another,
> And each one vanishes back where it came from
> Till all his hatchwork has been laid to rest.
> He comes to the footlights, gaping for applause,
> And except for the pink, withdrawn, quivering tongue,
> We see his mouth is absolutely empty.
>
> (152)

Not one to be timid about even the most outrageous pun, Wagoner's protagonist "eggs us on / To laugh and gag for him, to cluck and crow / For the last things we expected or hoped for." Like the snake chewing away on its tail, the magical eggs come full circle, disappear into themselves—and the magician, like the poet or the tricky contemporary novelist à la John Barth, is left speechless, emptied of his goods, twinkling.

To be sure, that something apparently pops out of nothing is the essence of the magician's artifice, and Wagoner retains a fascination for such images. Occasionally (as in "Laughter in the Dark," in *Riverbed* a poem based on the title of a Vladimir Nabokov novel and dedicated to that consummate trickster) dark shadows have an uncanny way of sliding across a lesson in what Wagoner calls "physics, good taste, and raw anatomy." "The First Law of Motion," in *Riverbed,* is a good example of the phenomenon. At first, the poem seems to be so much wit generated by a line from Newton's *Principia Mathematics* that serves as the epigraph: "Every body [Newton claims] perseveres in its state of rest, or of uniform motion in a right line, unless it is compelled to change that state by forces impressed thereon." Wagoner's reply—twenty-seven lines of poetry in constant motion, with nary a full stop in sight—begins like this:

> Staying strictly in line and going
> Along with a gag or swinging
> Far out and back or simply wheeling
> Into the home-stretch again and again,
> ‘not shoving or stalling, but coasting
> And playing it smooth, pretending
> To make light of it, you can seem
> To be keeping it up forever, needing
> Little or nothing but your own
> Dead weight to meet
> The demands of momentum . . .
>
> (174)

The poem's inertia is, of course, reflected in its rhythm and in the puns on death that seem to lurk around every speeding corner: ". . . you're going to be / Slowing down because turning / A corner means coming to a dead / Halt. . . ." Indeed, that is part of Wagoner's playful point—that "keeping time / Is as inhuman as the strict first law / Of motion."

Even when Wagoner is essentially engaged in send-up, in the periodic romp, he can still find a way to make sure that death has his entrance, and the last laugh. In "A Victorian Idyll," for example, a line from Emily Post's *Etiquette* ("A gentleman always falls behind his wife in entering the drawing room. . . .") is all he needs to send calculating puns in every direction:

> She came through the room like an answer in long division,
> At the top of her form, trailing a dividend.
> And when her husband fell down, as he always does,
> Flat on his face behind her and met the rug
> Like an old friend, we simply sharpened our charcoal.
>
> (154)

The resulting portrait captures that Victorian sense of decorum and decent gentility Wagoner is out to spoof:

> . . . A few included him
> In their sketches as an ambiguous portion
> Of the water, but the rest got down to business,
> Draping white samite over her rich shoulders
> And drawing the sword from their imaginations.
>
> (154)

In this case, however,"drawing" is a word worked hard—beyond its pun on sketching/pulling until it also includes the shivery suggestion that this is a sword that will be drawn across the proper Victorian lady's rich, creamy shoulders. Granted, the poem is an "idyll" (as well as an "idle") thought, the dark joke is there all the same.

In "A Valedictory to Standard Oil of Indiana" *(Staying Alive)* the satire turns vitriolic as well as dark. The jibes against the Company and what it does to Company towns and to Company people are standard enough:

> The word goes out: With refined regrets
> We suggest you sleep all day in your houses shaped
>   like lunch buckets
> And don't show up at the automated gates.
>
> (82)

In short, Standard Oil is, in Wagoner's bitter words, "canning my classmates."

But there is more: this is the poem he offers, in lieu of attending a high school reunion, "not from the hustings or barricades / Or the rickety stage where George Rogers Clark stood glued to the wall"; rather, the lines are as much about his stuck classmates as it is about the oily world that has slipped them up. And so, Wagoner—finally—offers his lines from "another way out" (the life of an artist? or, perhaps more to the point, the life of a *con* artist) "like Barnum's 'This Way to the Egress,' / Which moved the suckers when they'd seen enough. Get out of town."

A penchant for the quasi-didactic, for poetry-as-instruction (or is it, rather, instruction-as-poetry?) links ostensibly scattered strands of the Wagoner canon into something akin to a cohesive vision. "Staying Alive," for example, is built on a substructue of wilderness survival techniques; indeed, Wagoner was delighted when the poem was reprinted as a pamphlet and distributed to hikers. Hemingway had a similar experience when sections of "Big Two-Hearted River" were

printed in a camping magazine. It is no easy feat to describe how one
ought properly to pitch a tent or to bait a hook.

Nonetheless, the poetic substructure of "Staying Alive"—for all its
specificity, for all its attention to concrete detail—is still substructure. Wagoner has larger resonances in mind when he writes, for example, about those odd, unexpected moments that can happen even
while one is utterly "lost":

> . . . There may even come, on some uncanny evening,
> A time when you're warm and dry, well fed, not thirsty,
> Uninjured, without fear,
> When nothing, either good or bad, is happening.
> This is called staying alive. It's temporary.
>
> (55)

Or at those moments when knowing the correct signal is tantamont
to rescue:

> You should have a mirror
> With a tiny hole in the back for better aiming, for reflecting
> Whatever disaster you can think of, to show
> The way you suffer.
> These body signals have universal meaning: If you are lying
> Flat on your back with arms outstretched behind you,
> You say you require
> Emergency treatment; if you are standing erect and holding
> Arms horizontal, you mean you are not ready;
> If you hold them over
> Your head, you want to be picked up. Three of anything
> Is a sign of distress. Afterward, if you see
> No ropes, no ladders,
> No maps or message falling, no searchlights or trails blazing,
> Then, chances are, you should be prepared to burrow
> Deep for a deep winter.
>
> (55–56)

Notice how he uses, even exploits, the end position of words like "re-
flecting" or "lying" to pull the poem into wider, deeper directions.
Granted, punning is part of the process, but in his better poems,
puns are not an end in themselves.

In poems like "Do Not Proceed Beyond This Point Without a

Guide" *(Riverbed)* ("The hemlock had more sense. It stayed where it was, / . . . Being a guide instead of needing one.") or "The Other Side of the Mountain" ("To walk downhill you must lean partially backwards, / Heels digging in . . .") much of this spirit continued. Often, northwestern landscapes operate as a backdrop, almost as if by osmosis. But, in general, these are poems that owe their life to connections made, to metaphors established, from the flotsam and jetsam of contemporary life. What has become, for Wagoner, a congenial mode, one way to work his poetic magic, is not limited to a single analogy between woodsy advice and larger truths. The dramatic situation of objective instructor and wry detachment allows for that sense of quiet astonishment that infuses much of his best work. It is, I would submit, the stuff of magic, whether one encounters it on stage, in the forest, and, as so often happens, in the relentless absurdities of everyday life. Readiness, indeed, is all. The found situations become the germ of the "occasional" poem in much the way that other contemporary poets prided themselves on "finding" a poem by rearranging the lines on the back of a cereal box or on the instructions for taking a laxative.

When, for example, a police recruit (asked by NBC News why he likes his new job) claims that "it's not too much of a dull moment, and I'm not in one place at one time," the combination of shoddy speech and unwitting comedy provides Wagoner with an epigraph for a poetic monologue entitled "A Police Manual." What follows is a chilling lesson in standard operating procedures, one that might have been delivered by some sergeant plucked out of a Henry Reed poem (e.g., "The Naming of Parts") and issued GI togs and an American accent:

> The efficient use of a nightstick as an extension
> Of your arm and armor
> Lies at the heart of patrolling: each human body
> Has tender and vulnerable places whose location,
> By trial and error,
> You may find to your advantage.
>
> (156)

Because poetry *slows us down* as readers, because each word is chosen for its precision and, consequently, is weighed with more care than casual speech, what the instructor says bristles with dark possibilities.

To be sure, Wagoner is pulling the invisible strings, so his mario-
nette—or floating bulb, if you prefer a more magical allusion—moves
where he wants it to. This includes, for example, the concluding lines
that presumably mince no words about how to get on the "take":

> No news is good news. The bulk of your daily labors
> Will involve the crisp amusements and temptations
> That all men long for,
> The action, the power, the pursuit of unhappiness.
> Fives, tens, and twenties, up to half a dozen
> Can be folded over
> To the size of a matchbook; but the seemingly drab
> colors
> Are instantly recognizable from a distance.
> The trouble, therefore
> Is not in finding adequate compensation, but keeping it
> From showing too clearly. The rest is in your hands
> As a credit to the force.
>
> (156)

"Found epigrams" keep cropping up in Wagoner's canon, but he
can weave equally disturbing, shivery poems from, say, an unlikely
source such as the *International Code of Signals:*

> I cannot save my vessel.
> Keep as close as possible.
> I wish some persons taken off.
> A skeleton crew will remain on board.[6]

Thus far I have characterized Wagoner's reading as tilted toward
the quirky side (often the result of research for a novel-in-progress or
because Wagoner has always regarded reading as an all-consuming,
extracurricular activity), but he is anything but the dilettante. Indeed, his students would be quick to disabuse anybody of the notion,
especially when he begins to sniff the effete, the precious, or the un-
disciplined in his workshops. Talk with him about a book like *Who
Shall Be the Sun?* (1978) and it soon becomes clear that he "knows"
about Franz Boaz's anthropological investigations or about John R.
Swanton's literal transcriptions of Indian myths done for the Bureau
of American Ethnology—and, moreover, that he knows them deeply,
and well. Like the artifacts, Northwest Indian or otherwise, that poke

out of, or are piled near, every nook and cranny in Wagoner's house, this abundant stuff is not so much clutter. His is, in short, hardly a Victorian drawing room.

Rather, it is a place where spirits abide, in ways that both Blake and the Indians Wagoner often writes about would approve. Consider, for example, this poem from *Sleeping in the Woods* (1974):

Song for the First People

When you learned that men were coming, you changed into rocks,
Into fish and birds, into flowers and rivers in despair of us.
The tree under which I bend may be you,
That stone by the fire, the nighthawk swooping
And crying out over the swamp reeds, the reeds themselves.
Have I held you too lightly all my mornings? . . .

Let me become Water Dog, Bitterroot, or Shut Beak.
Change me. Forgive me. I will learn to crawl, stand, or fly
Anywhere among you, forever, as though among great elders.

                                                          (244)

For a poet who prefers sly matter-of-factness to airy metaphysics, who generally insists that his poems be grounded in the naturalistic here-and-now, there is a side of Wagoner that is very *immanentistic* indeed. I belabor the point because it is the mystical reverence for the world—and particularly for the Northwest—that energizes the songs and songlike poems or *Sleeping in the Woods,* as well as an impressive section of *New Poems* (1976).

Wagoner, of course, hardly needs anthropological arguments to convince him that the poet, the magician, and the shaman are first cousins. His recent poems in the "For a Woman . . ." series (*Landfall,* 1981) are, in effect, *charms,* attempts to exorcize or to otherwise cure through language's power. Here, in its entirety, is "For a Woman Who Said Her Soul Was Lost":

You wept past midnight like a ghost in an old novel,
Haunting a room, a stairway, a whole house with your half-dreaming
Pain, inconsolable, unable to hear me. Love, I confess
I took your soul into the woods, into the mountains
Early this morning, climbed a steep path with it,
Cold and deserted, stood with it among swordferns
And blossoming red currant where, together, we heard the wrens

And ruby-crowned kinglets reclaiming their worlds
From the melting winter as certainly as moonrise
While your lost body, miles away, wandered among doctors.
Sleep soundly, slowly, and softly now. Your soul is waiting
Here in safekeeping through a long, disembodied nightwatch.[7]

We do not need either to identify or to belabor the "source" of Wagoner's woman. No doubt his biographer will do exactly that, in ways that will satisfy curiosities at the same time it diminishes the poem per se. Perhaps it is best to let the lines stand as a testament to his lyrical gift, and to the personal stake in his poems. For the bald truth is that Wagoner's "magic," at its best, its richest, turns lyrical. If his poetry has a brittle edge, if his sardonic wit seems more appropriate to the New Yorker than to the Pacific Northwest, it is also worth remembering that his poetry has a consoling, a healing power. In "For a Woman . . ." sleight of hand is less important than summoning up the voice—and the words—required to confront the ghosts of the heart.

As he says in the final lines of a poem written shortly after his father's death:

> . . . He won't come back
> At anyone's bidding in his hard-hat of a helmet,
> His goggles up like a visor, but I dream him
> Returning unarmed, unharmed. Words, words. I hold
> My father's ghost in my arms in his dark doorway.[8]

As always, the premise of a Wagoner poem is crucial. It sets the dramatic situations, measures out carefully the canvas his words will fill. In this case, the epigram is to a midwestern folk belief that "If you count nine stars and nine stones, then look into an empty room, you'll see a ghost." One imagines, say, Tom Sawyer raised on precisely such magical notions, but Wagoner takes them—and magic—seriously. They are the threads he weaves into the extraordinary poetry we have come to expect.

Chapter Five
Concluding Remarks

If the old formula that goes "tell 'em what you're going to say, say it, then tell 'em what you said" is true, this is the point where I should come clean, and clear, about Northwest poetry. Is there such an animal? Does it really swim upstream to spawn or collect moss on the north side of its back? What, precisely, are its earmarks?

One response is to remember what Louis Armstrong used to say about jazz—namely, if you have to ask, you'll never know. Or what Stan Kenton used to quip when reporters asked him "where jazz was going": "Next week I'm in Cleveland." The "tests" for Northwest poetry are something like that—a feel for the landscape, a sense that the Northwest is as remote from the hot center of New York City as one can imagine, that such isolation can be bracing and meditative, as well as alienating and terrible.

To be sure, Northwest poets are not the only ones who alternately embrace and discourage a regional identification. Currently, Texas writers are lining up their guns in a range war about who is, or is not, an authentically "Texas" writer. As A. C. Greene points out, on the front page of the *New York Times Sunday Book Review* no less, "There is a genteel, but not always gentle, literary war going in Texas, fought, discretely of course, on several fronts under several banners."[1] Greene goes on to quote from an article by Don Graham, a professor of English at the University of Texas—Austin, published in the *Texas Humanist,* and, in the process, he washes a considerable amount of dirty Texas longjohns in widely public print:

The palefaces [Graham points out, borrowing his metaphor from Philip Rahv's famous distinction between the competing sensibilities of our national literature] are all those folks who stand ready to rescue Texas writing (and indeed Texas itself) from its provincial and nativisitic roots. Many of the Palefaces [e.g., Philip Lopate, Rosellen Brown, Stanley Plumley, etc.] are emigrés, recent arrivals, but many are homegrown, too . . . the literary equivalent to yuppies: upscale, well-educated, fern-bar writers.

At issue in Texas is nothing less than the ability of its once oil-rich universities (principally the University of Houston and Rice) to attract the brightest and the best to their campuses—and the predictable pinch as the "locals" feel displaced and unappreciated. A writer like, say, Donald Barthelme may have been born in Houston, but he has been for so long attached to the New York scene—and to the *New Yorker* magazine—that one would be hard-pressed to find his "Texanness." That he has returned to his alma mater, the University of Houston, tells us much about literary economics, maybe even something important about literary politics, but virtually nothing about literature itself.

After introducing the principal players and their "sides," Greene says this:

> The literary squabble between Houston and the rest of Texas, and Texas and the rest of the world, is not the real problem with Texas letters. The major issue concerns the creative act itself: Is there such a thing as "Texas writing"? Are there "Texas writers"? . . . The person readers today think of as the most important Texas writer is Mr. [Larry] McMurty, who wavers between accepting the designation and denying that it exists. In a 1981 scalping raid, that reached the public by way of *The Texas Observer,* Mr. McMurty surged across the border of his native state, flying such blood-banners as "There has never been a great Texas writer . . . Texas literature is disgracefully insular and uninformed." Castigating every Texas writer who does not pay attention to urban change, he pronounced "the country—western or cowboy—myth has served its time and lost its potency [and is] an inhibiting, rather than a creative, factor, in our literary life. The death of the cowboy [has] been lamented sufficiently, and there [is] really no more that need be said about it." Then, this year Mr. McMurty produced his massive novel, *Lonesome Dove,* which not only reverts to cowboys and cattle drives of the 19th century, but is peopled by a cast of Texans straight out of a video series (which it will very likely become).

As usual, Texas is America writ large. What the redskin writers in Texas hanker for—indeed, energized regional writers, good and bad, anywhere—is a sense that national magazines like *Time* and *People,* TV and radio, franchised food and suburban malls, have not homogenized *everything,* that there are still pockets where the people and their language, the landscape and its rhythms, remain relatively untouched.

Writers, of course, have special hankerings in addition to the ones already mentioned—that their work has a context, that it can form a version of *community,* with the shared vision and purpose that characterized the southern agrarians who clustered around John Crowe Ransom's *Kenyon Review,* the New England poets who followed in Robert Frost's flinty footsteps, or the New York intellectuals who made up the *Partisan Review* crowd. If this smacks of nostalgia, pure and simple, it is worth remembering that nostalgia is *never* pure and simple.

It is also worth remembering that criticism, as much as poetry, accounted for the cohesiveness and eventual "national" reputation of the southern agrarians. And in a similar way, it was the combination of Delmore Schwartz's brilliant essays and his poetry that helped establish his reputation as the definitive New York Jewish intellectual. For better or worse, Stafford, Hugo, and Wagoner have made their respective marks as poets, and in an age when the deconstructionists are always hunting about for thick poetic texts to "deconstruct," theirs has not been an especially easy lot.

In the same way that literary modernism could not survive its "success"—that is, the incorporation of Eliot, Joyce, Lawrence et al. into university curricula—creative writing programs have succeeded well beyond their wildest expectations. A heavyweight poet in residence now matters greatly to American colleges and universities, even if these same poets are largely ignored by the general public. In short, what was unthinkable only a few generations ago—namely, that a poet could pull down $75,000 per annum teaching a couple of workshops—has become a very palpable fact of poetic life. And so too has the mobility that comes with this giddy, high-priced territory. "Regionalism," in short, no longer stands still, because it no longer *has* to.

In this sense, Roethke was one of the trailblazers. No doubt there were local Northwest poets when he arrived—and, no doubt, they were jealous of his increasing fame—but it is one of literary history's harder truths that the third- and fourth-raters tend to be forgotten. What we remember is Roethke, and we remember him as a distinctively Northwest poet. No matter that he was born in Michigan and, I would add, no matter that William Stafford was born in Kansas or David Wagoner in Indiana. True, of the three poets I've concentrated on in this study, only Richard Hugo was born in the Pacific Northwest and only Hugo celebrated his northwestern identification without ambivalence or reservation. Still, the magazine Wagoner has edited for more than twenty-five years—*Poetry Northwest*—has done much to strengthen our sense of a Pacific Northwest with a "voice" and an aesthetic distinctly its own. If it is true, for example, that William Stafford retains much of his midwestern heritage, it is equally true that the sheer "wisdom" of his poetry owes much to the years he spent in Oregon.

Moreover, the Pacific Northwest has become a congenial place to work, and to write about, for dozens of first-rate poets—for Caroline Kizer and Tess Gallagher, for Kenneth O. Hansen and William Matchett—and, just as important, for those younger poets who show great promise. Consider, for example, these lines from Matthew Hansen's "Still Alive":

> . . . Cormorants dive
> in fog, fly low like snakes
> full of fish. This one dries
> his wings on piling at Port
> Townsend.
>
> I am still alive, doing fifty
> on the Aurora Bridge. Cloud breaks
> the white houses of Ballard
> shine, they shine.[2]

Granted, Hansen did not intend, nor does his poem support, a "reading" that would turn his delicate lines into a statement about the present condition of Pacific Northwest poetry. But in the context of this study, it seemed a proper note on which to end.

More claims than these a critic probably should not make, more categories than these would not be especially useful. The rest is not silence, but, rather, the hope that the poetry of Stafford, Hugo, and Wagoner speaks eloquently for itself—as an expression of the Pacific Northwest, and of the larger human condition embodied there.

Notes and References

Chapter One

1. David Wagoner ed., *Straw for the Fire: From the Notebooks of Theodore Roethke, 1943–63* (New York: Anchor Press/Doubleday, 1974), 205.
2. *The Collected Poems of Theodore Roethke* (New York: Anchor Press/Doubleday, 1975), 35.
3. Roethke would later insist, in "How to Write Like Somebody Else," that the line was "a fib. I had been reading deeply in Raleigh, and in Sir John Davies; and they rather than Willie [Butler Yeats] are the true ghosts in that piece."
4. See Ralph Mills, ed., *On the Poet and His Craft: Selected Prose of Theodore Roethke* (Seattle: University of Washington Press, 1965), 62.

Chapter Two

1. "Into the Cold World," in *Writing the Australian Crawl* (Ann Arbor: University of Michigan Press, 1978), 157.
2. *Stories That Could Be True: New and Collected Poems* (New York: Harper & Row, 1977), 193. All quotations from Stafford's poetry are from this edition. Hereafter page references are cited in the text.
3. "A Statement on Life and Writings" in *Writing the Australian Crawl,* 9.
4. From the transcript of a reading at Franklin and Marshall College, 15 April 1973.
5. "Statement on Life and Writings," 9.
6. "Finding Out What the World is Trying to Be: An Interview with Sanford Pinsker," in *Writing the Australian Crawl,* 114.
7. *Life Studies* (New York: Farrar, Straus and Giroux, 1959), 89.
8. Jonathan Holden, *The Mark to Turn* (Lawrence/Manhattan/Witchita: University Press of Kansas, 1976), 61.
9. "Finding Out What the World is Trying to Be," 115.
10. Holden, *The Mark to Turn,* 70–71.
11. "On Being Local," *Northwest Review* 13, no. 3 (1973):92.
12. "Finding Out What the World is Trying to Be," 117.
13. Richard Howard, *Alone in America* (New York: Atheneum, 1971), 504.
14. "Finding Out What the World is Trying to Be," 114.
15. Laurence Lieberman, *Unassigned Frequencies* (Urbana: University of Illinois Press, 1977), 268.

    16. Holden, *The Mark to Turn,* 30.
    17. "Finding Out What the World is Trying to Be," 120.

Chapter Three

    1. Thomas Gardner, "An Interview with Richard Hugo," *Contemporary Literature* 22, no. 2 (Spring 1981):152.
    2. Letter from Hugo, 7 August 1980.
    3. Gardner, "Interview," 151–52.
    4. *AWP Newsletter,* April 1980, 1.
    5. Donna Gerstenberger, *Richard Hugo,* Western Writers Series, no. 59 (Boise: Boise State University, 1983), 21. This volume provides invaluable information about Hugo's life and the locales he wrote about.
    6. *Making Certain It Goes On* (New York: W. W. Norton, 1984), 3; hereafter page references cited in the text.
    7. *The Triggering Town: Lectures and Essays on Poetry and Writing* (New York: W. W. Norton, 1979), 40; hereafter cited in the text as *TT* with page number.
    8. Gerstenberger, *Richard Hugo,* 16.
    9. Howard, *Alone in America,* 233.
    10. Gerstenberger, *Richard Hugo,* 21.
    11. Ibid., 24.
    12. Ibid., 25.
    13. Gardner, "Interview," 149.
    14. Ibid., 151.
    15. Ibid., 145–46.
    16. Ibid., 146.
    17. *The Collected Poems of Theodore Roethke,* 194.

Chapter Four

    1. *Collected Poems, 1956–1976* (Bloomington: Indiana University Press, 1976), 53; hereafter page references cited in the text. All quotations are from this edition unless otherwise stated.
    2. Letter from Wagoner to Pinsker, 4 August 1980.
    3. Sanford Pinsker, "On David Wagoner," *Salmagundi,* no. 22 (Spring–Summer 1973), 306.
    4. Robert Peters, "Thirteen Ways of Looking at David Wagoner's New Poems," *Western Humanities Review* 35 (Autumn 1981):267–68. Subsequent references to Peters are to this review-essay.
    5. Richard Hugo, "David Wagoner—A Poet of Elizabethan Wisdom and Wit," *Weekly's Reader: Seattle's Monthly Book Review,* November 1979, 1.
    6. "In Distress," in *Landfall* (Boston: Little, Brown and Company, 1981), 41.

7. *In Broken Country* (Boston: Atlantic Monthly Press, 1979), 29.
8. "My Father's Ghost," in *Landfall,* 15.

Chapter Five

1. A. C. Greene, "The Texas Literati: Whose Home Is This Range, Anyhow?" *New York Times Book Review,* 15 September 1985, p. 3. Subsequent reference to Greene are to this article.
2. Matthew Hansen, "Still Alive," *New Yorker* 17 February 1986, 34.

Selected Bibliography

William Stafford

PRIMARY SOURCES

1. Poetry
Traveling Through the Dark. New York: Harper & Row, 1962.
The Rescued Year. New York: Harper & Row, 1966.
Allegiances. New York: Harper & Row, 1970.
Someday, Maybe. New York: Harper & Row, 1973.
Stories That Could Be True. New York: Harper & Row, 1977.
A Glass Face in the Rain. New York: Harper & Row, 1982.

2. Interviews and essays
Writing the Australian Crawl: Views on the Writer's Vocation. Ann Arbor: University of Michigan Press, 1978.

SECONDARY SOURCES

French, Warren. " 'Sunflowers Through the Dark': The Vision of William Stafford." In *Late Harvest,* edited by Thomas Killoren, 179–90. Kansas City. BkMk press, 1977. A highly readable personal essay arguing that for all his years in the Pacific Northwest, William Stafford remains a "plains poet."
Holden, Jonathan. *The Mark to Turn A Reading of William Stafford's Poetry.* Lawrence: University Press of Kansas, 1976. The first book-length study of Stafford's poetry. While some of the "close readings" may be strained, the book is a valuable overview of Stafford's themes and techniques.
Lynch, Dennis Daily. "Journeys in Search of Oneself: The Metaphor of the Road in William Stafford's *Traveling Through the Dark* and *The Rescued Year.*" *Modern Poetry Studies,* 7 (1976):122–131. Divides the journey motif of Stafford's poetry into "three major archetypal areas: journeys of remembrance (concerned with past events), journeys of quest (concerned with future events), and journeys of experience (concerned with present events)."

Stitt, Peter. "William Stafford Wilderness Quest." In *The World: Hiero-glyphic Beauty: Five American Poets,* 57–88. Athens: University of Georgia Press, 1985. A first-rate chapter that explores the nature of Stafford's "spontaneous creativity" and his stature as a "wisdom poet."

Richard Hugo

PRIMARY SOURCES

1. Poetry
The Lady in Kicking Horse Reservoir. New York: Norton, 1973.
What Thou Lovest Well, Remains American. New York: Norton, 1975.
31 Letters and 13 Dreams. New York: Norton, 1977.
White Center. New York: Norton, 1980.
The Right Madness on Skye. New York: Norton, 1980.
Making Certain It Goes On: The Collected Poems of Richard Hugo. New York: Norton, 1983.

2. Fiction
Death and the Good Life. New York: St. Martin's press, 1981.
The Hitler Diaries. New York: Morrow, 1983.

3. Essays
The Triggering Town Lectures and Essays on Poetry and Writing. New York: Norton, 1979.

SECONDARY SOURCES

Allen, Michael S. *We Are Called Human: The Poetry of Richard Hugo.* Fayette-ville: University of Arkansas Press, 1982. Essentially a recasting of Allen's disertation, the book argues that Hugo is an heir—albeit, a radical one—to a western literary tradition that gives us men "who have valued the physical above and emotional, the big above the necessary, the tough above the humane."
Garber, Frederick. "On Richard Hugo and William Stafford." *American Poetry Review* 9, no. 1 (1980):16–18. An indispensable review of Hugo's *31 Letters and 13 Dreams* and Stafford's *Stories That Could Be True* that shows how the landscape of the Pacific Northwest becomes, for each, "a means of speaking of the landscape of the self."

Gerstenberger, Donna. *Richard Hugo.* Boise: Boise State University, 1983. Discusses Hugo's canon in the context of western writing. Especially valuable as an overview and for its biographical information.

Lindholt, Paul J. "Richard Hugo's Language. The Poem as 'Obsessive Musical Deed.' " *Contemporary Poetry* 16, no. 2 (Fall 1983):67–75. Applies Otto Jesperson's work in linguistics to Hugo's penchant for regional idiom and contemporary slang.

David Wagoner

PRIMARY SOURCES

1. Poetry

Staying Alive. Bloomington: University of Indiana Press, 1966.

Collected Poems, 1956–1976. Bloomington: University of Indiana Press, 1966.

Landfall. Boston: Little, Brown & Co., 1981.

2. Fiction

The Escape Artist. New York: Farrar, Straus, Giroux, 1965.

Where is My Wandering Boy Tonight? New York: Farrar, Straus, Giroux, 1970.

The Hanging Garden. Boston: Little, Brown & Co., 1980.

3. Edited Volume

Straw for the Fire: From the Notebooks of Theodore Roethke, 1943–1963. New York: Doubleday, 1972.

SECONDARY SOURCES

Boyers, Robert. "The Poetry of David Wagoner." *Kenyon Review* 32 (Spring 1970:176–81. An influential review that identifies *Staying Alive* as the point where Wagoner "really came into his own as a poet" and began to lay claims as a major figure.

Howard, Richard. "David Wagoner." In *Alone with America: Essays on the Art of Poetry in the United States since 1950,* 619–38. New York: Atheneum, 1971. Surveys, and accounts for, Wagoner's achievement both as a successful poet and a successful novelist.

Kennedy, X. J. "Pelting Dark Windows." *Parnassus* 5 (Spring/Summer 1977):133–40. A distinguished poet himself, Kennedy showers Wagoner with high praise, especially on the grounds that "Wagoner is so readable a poet that, coming to him after, say, an evening with Pound's later *Cantos,* one practically has a twinge of Puritan guilt, and feels shamelessly entertained—refreshed instead of exhausted."

Lieberman, Laurence. "David Wagoner: The Cold Speech of the Earth." In *Unassigned Frequencies: American Poetry in Review 1964–1977,* 152–81. Urbana: University of Illinois Press, 1977. An intelligent, very useful discussion of the ways in which "the ground of common speech" is applied to a variety of settings and occasions in Wagoner's canon.

McFarland, Ronald E. "David Wagoner's Dynamic Form." *Contemporary poetry* 5, 2 (1983):41–49. A readable account of Wagoner's stylistics.

Pinsker, Sanford. "On David Wagoner." *Salmagundi* 22–23 (Spring 1973):306–14. An overview of Wagoner's canon, focusing on those elements that distinguish his work from the Confessional School.

Index